THE INFORMER

D1532378

Ireland Into Film

Series editors:
Keith Hopper (text) and Gráinne Humphreys (images)

Ireland Into Film is the first project in a number of planned collaborations between Cork University Press and the Film Institute of Ireland. The general aim of this publishing initiative is to increase the critical understanding of 'Irish' Film (i.e. films made in, or about, Ireland). This particular series brings together writers and scholars from the fields of Film and Literary Studies to examine notable adaptations of Irish literary texts.

Other titles available in this series:

The Dead (Kevin Barry)
This Other Eden (Fidelma Farley)
December Bride (Lance Pettitt)
The Field (Cheryl Temple Herr)
The Quiet Man (Luke Gibbons)

Forthcoming titles:

Nora (Gerardine Meaney)
The Butcher Boy (Colin MacCabe)
Dancing at Lughnasa (Joan Dean)

Ireland Into Film

THE INFORMER

Patrick F. Sheeran

in association with
THE FILM INSTITUTE OF IRELAND

First published in 2002 by
Cork University Press
Cork
Ireland

© Patrick F. Sheeran 2002

British Library Cataloguing in Publication Data
A CIP catalogue record for this book is available from the British Library.

ISBN 1 85918 288 7

Typesetting by Red Barn Publishing, Skeagh, Skibbereen

Printed by ColourBooks Ltd, Baldoyle, Dublin

Ireland Into Film receives financial assistance from
the Arts Council / An Chomhairle Ealaíon and the Film Institute of Ireland

For my sons, David and Marcos

CONTENTS

LIST OF ILLUSTRATIONS

Acknowledgements

The editors would like to thank Sheila Pratschke, Lar Joye, Michael Davitt, Luke Dodd, Dennis Kennedy, Kevin Rockett, Ellen Hazelkorn, Dan O'Hara, Niamh Moriarty, St Cross College and St Clare's International College (Oxford), the School of Irish Studies Foundation and the Arts Council of Ireland. Thanks also to Ben Cloney, Lee Murphy, Emma Keogh and the staff of the Irish Film Archive, Kristine Kruger (AMPAS), Patricia Pusinelli (F.-W.-Murnau Stiftung), Liffey Films, National Library of Ireland, Lady Killanin, Twentieth Century Fox and Warner Bros.

Special thanks to Nina Witoszek, Phil Sheeran, Lucy Tynan, Seán Ryder, Kevin Barry, Iognáid Ó Muircheartaigh, Gearóid Ó Tuathaigh and Cormac Ó Comhraí.

All images may be sourced from the Irish Film Centre Archive.

Editors' Note

Professor Patrick F. Sheeran died shortly after completing the manuscript of this book. He is sorely missed by his family, friends, colleagues and students. To those individuals and institutions who helped him in the preparation of this work we hope that its posthumous publication will serve as a thank you for any assistance rendered.

MYTHOGENESIS

Stories that Grow out of Stories

Oh well, so much has been done to The Informer *that another
little sting can't matter.*[1]

Thus wrote Liam O'Flaherty, resignedly, to his American companion
Kitty Tailer apropos complications with the folio edition of his most
popular novel. Doubtless O'Flaherty would regard it as a further sting
and indignity to have a critic inflict the neologism 'mythogenic'
(meaning 'productive in story') on *The Informer* (1925) – and indeed
on Willie Mhaidhc himself from Inis Mór. But the nonce term has
its uses, both to evoke an extraordinarily labile novel and an
adventurous, wayward life that was equally rich in folklore, legend
and lies.

Mythogenic texts yield multiple adaptations, versions, recreations
and renditions. To date there have been four films of *The Informer*
(Arthur Robison 1929, John Ford 1935, Jules Dassin 1968, Michael
Byrne 1992) and at least three stage versions in English (John
McGreevey 1949, Micheál MacLiammóir 1958, Thomas Murphy
1981). More piquant are the adaptations and versions that failed to
make it to the boards: a proposed dramatization by the great German
experimentalist Piscator, an American opera with the catchy title
Gypo!, an Ardmore Studio remake of Ford's film, with Robert
Mitchum in the lead, and a BBC television serialization. And there
must be many further adaptations in the fourteen-odd languages
into which the novel has been translated.

A mythogenic text obscures and obfuscates its own origins,
thereby leading to tall tales and, sometime later, scholarly confusion.

Plate 1. The Informer *(dir. Michael Byrne, 1992).*

Famously, O'Flaherty gave two contradictory accounts of the genesis and purpose of *The Informer* – though these accounts are not so greatly at variance with one another as is sometimes supposed. One is to be found in a rhapsodic letter to his mentor Edward Garnett, the other in his shameless autobiography *Shame the Devil* (1934). To Garnett, one of the foremost men of letters of the day, *The Informer* is presented as a serious work of art; to the reader of the auto-biography it is presented as a scam designed to make an ass of O'Flaherty's critics.[2] Now that the author's letters have been published we can follow in greater detail the slide from one evaluation to the other and have a clearer idea of what was at stake. O'Flaherty's reports on *The Informer* in progress add up to a mini case study on the fluctuating definitions of what constitutes literature at any one time and who decides. (In this case it was the publisher, Jonathan Cape.) As an aid to further confusion, early readers of the novel and audiences for the first two film versions were encouraged to believe that *The Informer* offered a privileged insight into the secret revolutionary underground – the Bolsheviks – in Dublin during the troubles. However, novel and films had as much to do with the troubles in Weimar Germany.

A mythogenic text is not necessarily well written or artistically satisfying in itself. While it is true that for much of his writing life O'Flaherty was popularly regarded as a scoundrel and his novels as abominations, there came a time (post the publication of *Dúil* in 1953) when to criticize his work was tantamount to being 'anti-national'. One of the few to write in the 1960s with atypical forthrightness on the then sensitive topic of Irish literature and revolution was the novelist Francis MacManus. This is what he had to say when comparing O'Flaherty's novel to Daniel Corkery's War-of-Independence collection of stories *The Hounds of Banba*:

> *The Informer* has been a more widely read, a more successful book but it is a romantic melodrama, a peg to hang a man on, against a grim and sordid Dublin background which is no more than a background. The people are puppets jerked and tossed about in a danse macabre in a story of almost animal violence. The speech is synthetic. The revolutionary organization in the story is Communist, more like something out of a bad German or Polish novel. Gypo Nolan, the Informer, is a sort of primeval Judas, more ape than man, and although he has been able to serve as an altar boy and work as a policeman – the old R.I.C. were not geniuses but they were disciplined and trained – he is presented as a brutal troglodyte in whose brain just two facts can make what the author calls 'that loud primeval noise which is the beginning of thought'. Yet Yeats considered this – and Mr Gilhooley –

> a great novel 'too full of abounding life to be terrible despite
> the subject'.[3]

This gives us a useful set of co-ordinates on the novel and its jerky puppetry from the perspective of 1960s 'high seriousness'. MacManus comes close to saying here that O'Flaherty does not know what he is writing about and his brief, formal critique is equally challenging. He raises serious questions that deserve consideration, though they have often been brushed aside.

As the slighting reference to 'romantic melodrama' indicates, MacManus wrote at a time when a clear demarcation between high and popular literature could be maintained with a confidence few could muster today. However, his equally dismissive quotation from the novel on the 'loud primeval noise which is the beginning of thought' does indicate an enduring problem with O'Flaherty's work. Bluntly, in terms of the high modernist standards to which he subscribed (O'Flaherty was an avid student of Conrad, Lawrence and 'the Russians'), stretches of his writing, parts of *The Informer* included, are atrocious. Or, as he preferred it, 'tripe'. From first to last, O'Flaherty was aware of the problem and there is an amusing anecdote on the subject recounted in one of his letters from 1969:

> I also met the painter Eoin Walsh, who told me a funny story
> about a literary row in a pub called Sheehans, myself being
> the absent subject of the row. 'It was fierce,' Walsh said,
> 'about half swore that you are the world's greatest writer and
> the other half swore with equal passion that you are the
> worst.' 'Who won?' I asked. 'What,' he shouted, 'those
> bastards wouldn't even try to pull a soldier off their sister.'[4]

It is always worth attempting the rescue of one's sister from the soldiers. We will try to deliver O'Flaherty from some of his detractors at least, by arguing that the operative mode of his work and its filmic derivatives is indeed melodrama – but melodrama understood anew as a valid,

Plate 2. Liam O'Flaherty.

well-developed alternative to realist and modernist strategies. It is in O'Flaherty's often unwilling cultivation of this dominant form of popular narrative that we find one pointer to the novel's almost charismatic appeal, for melodrama provides the best culture (in the biological sense) in which to grow the mythogenic. This is because of both the wildly heterogeneous sources from which the mode derives and its manifest inclination towards allegory and myth.

Apart from the context of melodrama, there is yet another way to understand some of the novel's mythogenic power. This is to be found in the psychoanalytical approach to crisis developed by René Girard. For Girard, the sacrifice of a victim, the ritualization of terror by singling out a scapegoat, is one of the major ways in which a society reconstructs its boundaries and displaces violence from within.[5] From this perspective, Gypo the informer emerges as a hero of the 'sacrificial crisis', the scapegoat whom it is necessary to offer up in order that the community be redeemed from its own violence.

Gypo Nolan has a compulsion to die at the foot of the cross, aligned by camera angle, music and montage with that great western sacrificial victim, Jesus Christ. If a film may rightly be regarded as in some sense a critique of the novel on which it is based, so too the historical context of its making can fill out our intuition of the original text's significance. Robison's 1929 version was made (albeit in England) at a time of great turbulence in his adopted Germany. Ford's was filmed during the Depression and in the course of a bitter struggle between writers and the studios in Hollywood. Jules Dassin directed his all-black cast in *Uptight!* shortly after the death of Martin Luther King Jr. and as new strains appeared in the civil rights movement. Finally, Michael Byrne shot his independent version in Dublin at a peak of sectarian violence in Northern Ireland. It is, of course, always possible to align a text with trouble of some sort, but it does seem to be the case that O'Flaherty's *Informer* has resonated well with a number of 'sacrificial crises' and perhaps even illuminated the dire ritual of their resolution. It is a pointer to the fact that the mythogenic is not just a quality inherent in a text but is rather the result of a transaction between text and audience. There is no better example of this than the RKO Radio version of *The Informer* directed by Ford. Here was a film lacking in the usual Hollywood appeal: no happy ending, no great love interest, a repellent protagonist. Yet it took off, first with the critics and then with the general public. One explanation is surely the appeal of a down-at-heel hero to radical intellectuals and cinemagoers during the latter end of the Great Depression in the States.

A mythogenic text is deeply unstable. As the deconstruction movement has taught us, all texts are unstable, full of holes and contradictions. But some texts are clearly more unstable than others – and may be none the worse for that. O'Flaherty's novel is riven by fertile contradictions in a number of areas, more especially in the tension between an ostensibly forward-driving realistic narrative and a static, tableau-like presentation of conflicting forces and ideas. The language too betrays a certain strain. There is the laconic delivery of the hard-boiled thriller side by side with the inter-title of the silent film, an occasional touch of Synge mixed in with O'Casey's Dublinese and perhaps even a grim animated cloud or two from Thomas Hardy. Depending on one's taste, this may be taken as mere synthetic speech (MacManus) or a rich polyglot *à la* Bakhtin's celebration of diversity of register and speech in the novel.

Two further areas of tension are worth attending to briefly at this point, as they have a bearing on the pattern of exchange between the fiction and the films: male gender and the actual historical time in which the novel is set.

With regard to the first, O'Flaherty has cast together, in the characters of Gypo Nolan and Commandant Dan Gallagher, two very different forms of masculinity that hardly belong to the same time or place. Gypo is pre-modern and, as the saying goes, politically illiterate. Gallagher, his antagonist, is hyper-modern and politically aware to the point of nihilism. Gypo harks back to the Faction Fighters of early nineteenth-century Munster and Ulster, for whom violence was largely recreational and an expression of sheer male vitality. Gallagher's nearest contemporaries belong to the Frei Corps in Bavaria, with all the pathology and ferocity of partisan commitment that the comparison implies. More, the characters themselves are internally divided: Gypo is an urban peasant, Commandant Gallagher a red fascist. Hence the dizzy range of possibilities open to a director in portraying these febrile characters on stage or screen.

One of the many virtues of *The Informer* as realist narrative is that it preserves a tight chronological sequence from three minutes to six in the evening to six the following morning. This is so much dust thrown in our eyes, however, insofar as it keeps us from enquiring into the actual historical time of the narrative itself. In the cinematic versions, that time has proved to be extraordinarily variable. So much is this the case that it is becoming hard to hold onto the fact that O'Flaherty's novel is actually about green-on-green violence in the period immediately *after* the Civil War. There is not a British soldier, Black and Tan or Auxiliary in sight. Or an IRA man for that matter. It is quite otherwise in the films.

In Robison's version the antagonists are 'the Party' and the police in a simulacra of the Weimar Republic. John Ford, indulging his Irish nationalist rather than his Empire enthusiast persona – *The Black Watch* (1929), *Four Men and a Prayer* (1938), – shifts the time of his film back to the War of Independence (1919–1921), when men were men and the British were very nervous. Dassin is, to a degree, true to the spirit of the novel when he restages *The Informer* (*Uptight!*) as black-on-black violence in Cleveland in the 1960s. Byrne's amateur version is the dullest, just because it attempts fidelity to the original – though here too there is a shift backwards in time to the War of Independence.

One plausible reason for tinkering with *The Informer* in this way is that an action set in the context of the IRA versus the Black and Tans was certainly felt to be more intelligible and clear-cut to cinema audiences than one where Irishmen shot their compatriots. The fantasy that the Civil War never happened was also a factor. But there is more at work here and there is a significant warrant for the time shifts within the novel itself.

One clue is in the opening sentence, which reads: 'It was three minutes to six o'clock in the evening of the fifteenth of March 192__'.[6] Minute detail is followed by a yawning gap. Is it – it can only be – 1922? Does it matter? Of course O'Flaherty is working up an air of mystery and of I-dare-not-tell-too-much-or-I'll-be-shot, in the manner of contemporary thriller writers – though there were paranoid moments when he felt he would indeed be shot for writing *The Informer*. His fellow writers generally used the dash to disguise a place rather than a date – as indeed the author does further down the page with his reference to 'B__ Road'.

It is worth following this clue a little further. If we shift our attention to the sketchy 'back story' of the novel, something of interest emerges. In this, Gypo Nolan and his sidekick Frankie McPhillip have been sent down the country by the Revolutionary Organization (*sic*) to aid with a farm labourers' strike. McPhillip shoots the secretary of the local branch of the Farmers' Union, goes on the run and, on his return to Dublin, is betrayed by Gypo. Insofar as these imaginary events can be given a local habitation and a name, we have to locate them in 1922 and in Tipperary. In the early months of the emerging Free State not only were there many strikes and occupations in the Irish countryside but rudimentary soviets were set up and some flew the red flag. The Dublin-based Communist Party of Ireland, of which O'Flaherty was a leading member, did nothing whatever to aid the rural activists. Quite the opposite. The communist paper the *Workers' Republic* reported the 'soviets' – and reprimanded them. Mike Milotte, the historian of communism in Ireland, notes regretfully:

> The novelist Liam O'Flaherty, then a prominent CPI member, dismissed the occupations as 'merely incidental to the everyday struggle against capitalism . . . not by any

means revolutionary, the workers are not acting beyond the bounds of capitalist production'. The party did not explain *how* it could develop and become powerful while standing aloof from the *actual* workers' struggles going on around it.[7]

No attempt, Milotte notes, was ever made to contact or recruit the leaders. The notion, then, of a Bolshevik 'Revolutionary Organization' in Dublin in the mid 1920s with active links to rural discontent as suggested in *The Informer* is pure compensatory fantasy. This is not for a moment to deny the novelist's right to imagine history as he pleases, but it is to suggest that later filmic distortions of the historical background to O'Flaherty's novel have a good precedent in the novel's own manipulations of the record.

As might be expected from the above, there are similar difficulties with the portrayal of the ideological clash between nationalism and communism in the book. O'Flaherty half solves the problem by equipping his Revolutionary Organization with Comintern policy and an IRA structure and *modus operandi*. As Commandant Gallagher admits in a rueful moment: 'They talk at International Headquarters about Romanticism and leftism and all sorts of freak notions. What do they know about the peculiar type of hog mind that constitutes an Irish peasant?'[8] His own romantic, not to say gothic, affiliations are hinted at when he remarks of the just escaped Gypo: 'That hulking swine can do his best. I will drain his blood before dawn.'[9] The image of Dracula in the popular imagination is a reminder of what happens to all great mythogenic texts and heroes. It is their fate to be replaced by later versions of themselves. Who, after Bela Lugosi and Frank Langella, cares to recall that Bram Stoker's original Count looked like a sewer rat, or (much less famously), after Victor McLaglen and Preston Foster, that Gypo and Gallagher fought one another more than they ever fought the Tans?

The Informer, then, has been a peculiarly enabling and disabling work. Far from being the best of O'Flaherty's novels (that title must go to *Skerrett*), it earned him great acclaim though very little money. The film adaptations, in turn, do not figure among the most important achievements of the directors concerned. Robison's *Schatten* ('*Warning Shadows*', 1922) is a major work of the German expressionist period and has a place in world cinema. His version of *The Informer*, though a very cinematic rendition, is not as accomplished as his work in Germany. Ford's version is something of an anomaly in an *oeuvre* that reached its peak in the cavalry trilogy. Oddly, his film is much more expressionist in technique than Robison's. Jules Dassin, director of the *noir* classic *Naked City* (1948), largely failed in his polemical attempt to apply O'Flaherty's fable to the black ghetto. Yet *Uptight!* was viewed as dangerously subversive in its time and evidence has since emerged that the FBI did all in their power to put a stop to the production. Even more extraordinary today is to read the contemporary reviews. One critic berated Dassin for basing his film on *The Informer* story and thereby setting up an implicit comparison between the noble history of the Irish struggle for independence and such a paltry thing as black insurgency in America's inner cities.[10] Such a distortion of a distortion offers final, perverse testimony to the mythogenic power of O'Flaherty's fiction.

Glancing over this farrago of fable and fantasy one is tempted to entertain yet another baleful deconstructive notion: perhaps there is no original here, either in history or in personal experience. Sure enough, O'Flaherty writes to Garnett in April 1924: 'I expect to go ahead with my novel now. I am going to try and sell it serially and for film. I think it would work well on the films at least.'[11]

Was it all a film in the first place?

There is a Borgesian history of the Irish troubles which could be written along the lines of the Argentinian master's *Thema del traitor y del hero* ('Theme of the traitor and the hero'). It would trace the approximate beginnings of the struggle to the summer of 1914 when Sidney Olcott, late of Kalem Films, provided the Irish Volunteers in Kerry with the prop-guns from the set of *Bold Emmet, Ireland's Martyr* for a parade. A basic premise of such a history would run that the Easter Rising, with its defence of fixed positions, was theatre, while the War of Independence and the Civil War, mobile and ever-changing in focus, were film. If Cuchulainn stalked through the Post Office with the men of 1916 as Yeats averred, then Tom Mix traversed the hills with the Flying Columns. One thing that both the scenographic and cinematographic versions of the Irish troubles held in common was a melodramatic vision of politics, with conventional roles for the maiden victim (Ireland), the brute villain (England or the Informer) and the brave hero (the Patriot). Nothing seems more ridiculous and laughable to one generation than the heightened actions and language that an earlier generation took for realism. Hence the ease with which revisionists have been able to rubbish popular versions of nationalist history.[12]

The Borgesian approach is tempting but flippant. It makes light of terrible deeds. In the first four months of 1921, J. Bowyer Bell informs us, in his history of the IRA, 'seventy-three bodies were found with a placard announcing the removal of a spy and informer'.[13]

The removal!

Staging Demonstrations

It is worth glancing, however perfunctorily, at O'Flaherty's involvement with radical politics in Ireland, if only because that involvement offers some further clues to the creative contradictions of *The Informer*.

In 1916, along with tens of thousands of his fellow countrymen, Liam O'Flaherty was a member of the British Army. In September 1917 he became shell-shocked while serving with the Irish Guards at Langemarck and invalided out the following year with what his medical record describes as *melancolia acuta*. He then embarked on two years of world travel and returned to Aran in 1920 at the height of the War of Independence. He took no part in the guerrilla campaign, either because he had become a communist or because he was suffering from a nervous breakdown (both reasons have been put forward on different occasions). In any event he might have had some difficulty in finding comrades-in-arms. Connemara was one of the least active areas during the war. After a visit to London, O'Flaherty returned to Dublin in December 1921 and joined Roderick Connolly's newly established Communist Party of Ireland, formerly the Socialist Party of Ireland. A month later, in January 1922, he declared himself 'Chairman of the Council of the Unemployed', seized the Rotunda at the north end of O'Connell Street with 120 men – many of them ex-soldiers – and ran up the red flag. Once in the Concert Hall of the Rotunda (a favourite location for showing films, incidentally: the first native feature film, *Ireland – A Nation*, had a brief screening there in 1917), O'Flaherty posted sentries, threw up barricades, drilled his men, reduced the more disorderly to the ranks and was himself styled the Commander-in-Chief. Leading members of the garrison posed under the red flag for a picture in the *Freeman's Journal*. Ominously, the caption to the newspaper photograph put 'garrison' in quotation marks. O'Flaherty 'held' the Rotunda for four days, after which he was allowed to make his way south to rebel Cork. Thereafter he claimed that he joined the Four Courts rising until disbanded in June 1922, at which point he returned to England in a trench coat with a revolver strapped between his shoulder blades . . . If all of this is true, it is quite a career for the young Irish Lenin from Gort na gCopall.

There is a streak of macho sentimentality in many literary historians of this period which leads them to identify with Republican gunmen on the run. By way of antidote and to defamiliarize approved sentiment, we can recall the famous observation of the much execrated Kevin O'Higgins, Minister for Home Affairs in the Provisional Government. That government, he recalled, was made up of 'simply eight young men in the City Hall standing amidst the ruins of one administration, with the foundations of another yet to be laid, and with wild men screaming through the keyhole'.[14] O'Flaherty was one of the wild men.

The red flag over the Rotunda has almost entirely escaped the history books (though a few specialized monographs on Irish labour mention it in passing). It has been passed over, and not out of the usual pettifogging desire to airbrush radical dissent from the record. The occupation was, in the language of paramilitaries then and now, a 'stunt', undertaken without the approval of the CPI who, deeply embarrassed, negotiated a safe passage out of the building for the unarmed, though well-fed, Red Guards and their commander. Even in January 1922 in Dublin the idea of taking over a public building, running up a flag, making a proclamation and expecting the people to rise up was *passé*, an imitation of an imitation of an imitation. Not that this deterred anybody determined to live in the nineteenth century before the deployment of heavy ordnance. Irish revolutionaries of the period are said to have been burdened with too much imagination. The reverse was often the case.

The extent of O'Flaherty's involvement with the Republicans holding the Four Courts in defiance of the Provisional Government is similarly open to question. There is a stagy account of mopping-up operations by Free State troops in *Shame the Devil*:

> It was O'Connell Street in Dublin, during the capture of the Republican headquarters by the Free State troops in June 1922. I was standing on the south side of the bridge with a comrade. We had been disbanded on the previous day and we were now watching the destruction of the hotels where headquarters were still holding out. The Free State soldiers were throwing incendiary bombs from across the street into the hotels. There was a rattle of machine-gun and rifle fire. A cordon had been thrown all around the doomed buildings and crowds of people stood outside the barriers, watching the scene, as at a public entertainment. Then I heard an old woman in a group behind me say: 'Did ye hear that bloody murderer Liam O'Flaherty is killed, thanks be to God?'

'Who?' said another woman.

'Liam O'Flaherty,' said the first. 'The man that locked the unemployed up in the Rotunda and shot them unless they spat on the holy crucifix. The man that tried to sell Dublin to the Bolsheviks.'

'Is he dead?' said a man.

'Shot through the heart this morning in Capel Street,' said the old woman. 'The Lord be praised for ridding the country of that cut-throat. Ho me hearties! Give the bastards what's coming to them.'[15]

This is mythogenesis at work on two fronts. It is also counter-revolution as theatre, a sub-O'Casey scene and not O'Flaherty's best genre. The 'we' of the first paragraph are the members of the CPI who did in fact throw in their lot with the Republicans once the fighting started. They could hardly do otherwise, since they had been urging the necessity of Civil War in the pages of the *Workers' Republic* for months. Roderick Connolly with a dozen men took over two hotels and exchanged a few shots with Free State troops. Sensibly, they abandoned their positions once the main assault began. But they did not disband, as O'Flaherty suggests. No group disbanded at this point: the war was only beginning. Mike Milotte sums up the Civil War involvement of the CPI:

> Despite numerous reports in the *Workers' Republic* over the past months to the effect that the CPI had a fully armed and trained 'Red Guard' under its control, its contribution to the actual fighting was minimal. No such organization existed, and in claiming that it did the communists simply hoped to persuade the IRA to take them more seriously.[16]

The vernacular form of mythogenesis is bluff.

When comparing O'Flaherty's high-flown vignettes with the historical record, it is tempting to reach for the weapon he himself proffers on the fly page of *Shame the Devil* (the inscription reads 'I Offer This Dagger To My Enemies'). But that would be to miss an important point. His whole sensibility, his way of apprehending and then portraying the world, was to invest events with heightened colour and intensity. Like Joseph Conrad, who turned an adolescent fit of depression and attempted suicide into a grand affair of passion and gallantry, O'Flaherty made the melodramatic most of his *melancolia acuta*. Two points emerge from any review of O'Flaherty's formative years. First, his outlook, his ideological commitments, even his psychology, were overwhelmingly a product of World War I. (He would even manage on occasion to be simultaneously anti-Semitic and anti-German, a cocktail of prejudice found largely east of the Elbe.) France and the trenches were decisive: 'I was brought in contact there with all manner of working men, French, English, British colonials and German prisoners with whom we talked both across the trenches and in the internment camps. I attribute the awakening of my conscious mind to this experience.'[17]

Second, his communist sympathies, also picked up in France during the war, inevitably put him at a tangent to the overwhelmingly nationalist struggle in Ireland. There were no more than twenty members of the CPI in Dublin in 1922. More to the point, O'Flaherty modelled the situation in Ireland in very un-Bolshevik terms. The country, he claimed, enjoyed 'Elizabethan conditions' though no Shakespeare had yet arrived on the scene.[18] With this very literary – and not unprecedented – assessment went an aestheticization of violence of a kind common in the emergent fascist movements in Europe. He was quite straightforward about this in a letter to the *Irish Statesman*:

> In Ireland, to my mind, we have reached that point in the progress of our race, the point which marked the appearance of Shakespeare in English Literature. Let us not be shamed that gunshots are heard in our streets. Let us be glad. For

force is, after all, the opposite of sluggishness. It is an intensity of movement, of motion. And motion is the opposite of death . . . Ours is the wild tumult of the unchained storm, the tumult of the army on the march, clashing its symbols, rioting with excess of energy. Need we be ashamed of it?[19]

Drawing up literary analogies is a risky business at the best of times; in retrospect, 1924 seems more Jacobean than Elizabethan, with O'Flaherty as its Cyril Tourneur. More importantly, despite his penchant for Elizabethan drama, he made a significant break with the then dominant theatrical trophing of contemporary history. *The Informer* is one of the first and most thoroughgoing examples of the new, consciously cinematic novel. By an odd coincidence, the Hollywood director who would best realize the cinematic potential of the book happened to be on a visit to the west of Ireland in December 1921 – the very month in which O'Flaherty returned from London to Dublin to foment revolution. The name on the visitor's passport was John A. Feeney. He claimed to have been born Sean Aloysius O'Fearna, was currently known professionally as Jack Ford, and would shortly be even better known as John Ford. He was twenty-seven years of age and had already directed over thirty feature films.

Ford and O'Flaherty met up in Hollywood thirteen years later and claimed to be cousins – presumably on the basis that Ford's mother was a Curran from Kilronan, Inishmore, and that all Aran Islanders were related somewhere along the line. Interestingly, Ford does not seem to have visited Aran on this trip but focused instead on Spiddal, from where his father, John Feeney, had emigrated to America in 1854. This visit during the truce was to be of signal importance in shaping the young director's attitude to Irish affairs. As one might expect from a man who was to gain the reputation of being the straightest liar in Hollywood, the visit grew to epic proportions, an

Plate 3. John Ford on location in Ireland.

elaboration eagerly aided and abetted by his Irish relatives. We can begin by bracketing the suggestions that he was on a secret 'mission' (an operative for American naval intelligence? a volunteer in the struggle for Irish freedom?) or that he was beaten up by the Black and Tans and ordered out of the country. The facts are strange enough.

The Mother of all Mythomaniacs

Shortly after the birth of his first son to Mary McBryde Smith, a daughter of Southern landed gentry, John Ford took ship to visit the land of his ancestors. He kept what he called a 'sort of diarrhoea' for his wife, and it is this diary-cum-letter which provides a fascinating insight into the workings of Ford's mind and into the perils of jumping to conclusions about what is fact, what fable. Three brief episodes from the diary will illustrate the point. There is first a finely cinematic description of a group of Irish priests saying mass on the deck of the liner as the ship passes up the Irish coast on the way to Liverpool: 'Just as the priest lifted the host, the clouds and fog lifted and three miles away we could see the shores of our beloved fatherland, "The Emerald Isle" as green and as fresh as dew on the down. Even the priest stopped . . . [and] gazed.'[20] This is quintessential Ford, with his piety, his eye for the climactic, communally satisfying moment, his compelling mixture of sentimentality and deeply felt allegiance. Anybody who has even the remotest experience of exile can hardly fail to respond. Next comes an episode which is surely an exemplary Fordian fiction. He takes the night mail-boat from Holyhead to Kingstown:

> The boat I travelled in across the Irish Sea carried Michael Collins and Arthur Griffith, the returning Sinn Féin delegates with Lloyd George's proposals to Dáil Eireann. We were only twenty minutes from Holyhead when we cut a fishing schooner in two and sank her. Three of the crew were drowned and although we cruised around for an hour we found no bodies. The shock of the impact was terrible. When we struck, the boat shivered and rocked for quite a while before she straightened out . . .[21]

This is the kind of thing that happens in fiction, not history. The ship carrying Michael Collins and the treaty proposals which will lead to a bloody civil war is involved in a premonitory fatal accident! *And* there is a sympathetic young American aboard to record the episode in voice-over. It reeks of the 'precipitating incident' so dear to the heart of Hollywood script doctors. Yet it happened just as Ford describes it – with minor emendations. Griffith was not on board; he had gone ahead the previous day to prepare for the Dáil meeting of 3 December 1921. Collins was accompanied by Gavan Duffy and Erskine Childers who did their best to reassure the frightened passengers. Ford seems to have missed Collins declaring: 'I have been in tighter corners than this.'[22] Next we come to Spiddal:

> At Galway I got a jaunting car and rode to Spiddal and had a deuce of a time finding Dad's folks. There are so many Feeneys out there that to find our part of the family was a problem. At last I found them . . . Spiddal is all shot to pieces. Most of the houses have been burned down by the Black and Tans and all the young men had been hiding in the hills . . . Cousin Martin Feeney (Dad's nephew) had been hiding in the Connemara Mountains with the Thornton boys. I naturally was followed about and watched by the Black and Tan Fraternity. Tell Dad that the Thornton house is entirely burned down and old Mrs Thornton was living with Uncle Ned's widow while his sons were away . . .[23]

Most of this is pure invention. No house in the village was burned down by the Black and Tans, though two or three in outlying districts were. Any incendiary activity in Spiddal was undertaken by the North Galway IRA, who burned down Lord Killanin's house. The East Connemara Brigade, in whose 'area' the village lay, had at most one or two guns, if any, and were not especially active during the War of Independence, though a number were indeed 'on the run' while hostilities lasted. Recall that Ford's visit occurred during the truce. What is going on here?[24]

There is a cruel, entirely apocryphal, story about Galway city which may shed light on the assertion that Spiddal was all shot to pieces. It goes that, during World War I, a German submarine commander entered Galway Bay, upped periscope and examined the city with a view to shelling it. He came to the conclusion that it was not worth the effort, since the place had plainly been shelled already. Perhaps the visitor from California drew similarly mistaken conclusions from the derelict condition of his father's natal village. Ford's reference to the Connemara 'Mountains' tells another story, however. There are no mountains around Spiddal, but 'mountain' is used in the Hiberno-English speech of the area to denote a piece of boggy upland, no more than a hundred feet above sea level. It is this combination of momentary, unnerving precision within a largely legendary framework that is often the hallmark of Ford's best work.

Whatever the truth about Spiddal, the visit to Ireland at the end of 1921 was a formative one for Ford. It entrenched his sense of Irishness, or, better, the peculiar kind of Irishness available at the time to a first-generation prosperous Irish-American brought up in the tradition of grievance. Thereafter he contributed funds all his life to the IRA. Equally telling is the fantasy Irish-self engendered by the visit which years later will figure in the rewrites of the script of *The Quiet Man* (1952). The original short story by Maurice Walsh (1933) concerns a returned emigrant who settles back in Ireland and marries the local beauty, Eileen O'Grady. Ford turned 'The Quiet Man' over to Richard Llewellyn, with instructions to expand it into a novella. The new revised version was to take place during the Tan war and the hero's homecoming was to be motivated by the desire to help his family and country. Subsequent script drafts by John and Frank Nugent made much of Black and Tan incursions and brutality in the village of Innisfree (i.e. Spiddal).

All these shenanigans were later dropped from the shooting script. The usual explanation offered is that the imported violence hardly fitted with the romantic, celebratory mood of the film. But one wonders. One of those involved with *The Quiet Man* was none other than Lord Killanin, whose home in Spiddal had been torched in 1922. Perhaps a more nuanced sense of the troubles and who-did-what-to-whom had begun to impinge on Ford's fantasy of himself as Irish-America's revenge for Cromwell. There is no doubt but that he remained a fervent Irish nationalist all his life, but again this was complicated by his equally fervent desire to be accepted by the WASP American establishment.

Albert Memmi, in his classic study *The Colonizer and the Colonized*, remarks in passing on the number of prominent North African nationalists who contracted mixed marriages with blonde daughters of the imperial power. He reads this as an attempt to resolve a simultaneous hatred and love for the oppressor.[25] Ford-as-Irish-nationalist fits this model of fraught colonized man rather well. He married into the conservative Presbyterian North Carolina gentry and thereafter many puzzling aspects of his career may be plausibly accounted for as attempts to impress (or flee from) a wife who regarded filmmaking as a 'low Irish' activity. His strange departure for Ireland shortly after his son's birth may be taken in this context as an effort to right the balance of competing allegiances. Just how far Ford was prepared to go in cultivating the 'Irish' side of his personality is shown by an interview he gave to the leading French cineaste Jean Mitry. Mitry had written one of the first and best studies of Ford but found himself compelled to admit an error in the book as a result of his personal interview with the great man. John Ford was not born in America, as he had earlier (and correctly) written, but in the west of Ireland in the region of Cong, where his brilliant new film was set.[26] With some precedent, the newspaper editor in *Who Shot Liberty Valance?* (1962), one of Ford's greatest works, famously asserts: 'When the legend becomes fact, print the legend.'

2

FILM INTO NOVEL INTO FILM

O'Flaherty's Native Art

So-called 'cinematic novels' can be very deceptive. Many were written, it turns out, before the cinema was invented or the author in question had actually seen a film. Just how cautious one needs to be about the carry-over of montage, cross-cutting, fragmentation, the 'dumb eye' of the camera, etc., into a particular fiction is shown by the following example:

> *Silhouettes* . . . described a row of mean little houses along which the narrator passes after nightfall. His attention is attracted by two figures in violent agitation on a lowered window-blind illuminated from within, the burly figure of a man, staggering and threatening with upraised fist, and the smaller sharp-faced figure of a nagging woman. A blow is struck and the light goes out. The narrator waits to see if anything happens afterwards. Yes, the window-blind is illuminated again dimly, by a candle no doubt, and the woman's sharp profile appears accompanied by two small heads, just above the window ledge, of children wakened by the noise. The woman's finger is pointed in warning. She is saying, 'Don't waken Pa'.

This, if not an actual scenario for a short film, must surely be written by an author familiar with the silent cinema, and probably with German Expressionism at that; perhaps he/she has even seen Robison's *Schatten* ('*Warning Shadows*'). As Alan Spiegel, who draws attention to *Silhouettes*, comments, the passage finds numerous equivalents for cinematic form – the window is seen from a particular

Plate 4. Schatten *(dir. Arthur Robinson, 1923).*

perspective, the visual field is fragmented, there is a temporal elision in the middle of the action and so on.[27]

The passage in fact comes from Stanislaus Joyce's memoir and concerns an early writing project planned by his brother James sometime in the 1890s – before there was a cinema in Dublin and almost certainly before James Joyce had seen a film of any kind.

If Joyce has been read and over-read in cinematic terms, O'Flaherty (a much lesser figure) has suffered from a different kind of misconstrual, one that emphasizes not the visual but the supposed oral, folk-tale substratum of his art. Denis Donoghue, in the course of his lucid preface to *The Informer*, notes O'Flaherty's oratorical and melodramatic inclinations and finally puts them down, where they have generally been put, to the folk tradition:

All his life he remained a teller of tales, more at home in the oral tradition than in the printed page. When we feel that his English style is in excess of its purpose and need, the reason is that O'Flaherty's native art is sanctioned more completely in the procedures of Irish oral narrative than in those of the modern English novel.[28]

While Donoghue acknowledges the influence of Dostoevsky and Conrad, he does not pause to consider that the excesses of O'Flaherty's 'native art' may derive their sanction from sources vastly more widespread and closer to hand than the oral traditions of Aran. However alluring it may be to propose a Gaelic provenance for the rhetoric of *The Informer*, the evidence points elsewhere: O'Flaherty's letters, published statements and the novel itself confirm that he had his eye on the silent cinema, and probably on the German expressionist cinema at that. The attempt to emulate in words the gestural language of the silents is what partly accounts for the work's excessive, grotesque quality. O'Flaherty was more at home in the cinema than on the printed page – or in the oral tradition.

The creative impact of cinema on fiction has usually been studied almost exclusively in terms of the formal innovations of such major modernist figures as Gertrude Stein, James Joyce, Virginia Woolf and John Dos Passos. The neglect of the creative exchange between image and word in the work of less strenuous figures such as O'Flaherty has led to a large misconception. It is to the effect that the seventh art and modernist literature were somehow allied in 'making it new', in breaking with the outworn conventions of an earlier era. The opposite is surely the case. As Charles Eidsvik pointed out thirty years ago: 'Modernist writing explicitly rejected the traditions of Victorian literature. Movies were a direct extension of Victorian tradition. Until recently, the art forms were essentially combatants, and if the cinema influenced modernist literature, it influenced it in a negative rather than a positive way.'[29] Though he does not mention it, the film script in *Finnegans Wake* goes some way towards supporting this contention.

Eidsvik's argument itself requires some revision in the light of more recent work on the continuity, integrity and importance of melodrama all through the modern period. However, it is worth having it in this trenchant form because it is just this notion that cinema and any strictly modernist mode of writing were at odds that is implicit in O'Flaherty's correspondence on *The Informer*. He knew he was writing a cinematic novel, but he wasn't particularly happy about it.

To understand the issues at stake for him we have to recall the extravagant hopes he had placed in his previous novel of 1924, *The Black Soul* – a novel virtually co-written with Edward Garnett. It was, he said, 'the song with which I hoped to storm the highest heavens'.[30] The highest heaven was the modernist literary firmament occupied just then by the expanding supernova of D. H. Lawrence (also a Garnett protégé). 'Song' too has its specific reference. O'Flaherty was a rhapsodic writer, exultant (and probably unbearable) when inspired, utterly bereft when the muse departed. Garnett steadied him, stylistically and otherwise, during the composition of *The Black Soul*.

The novel was a flop. O'Flaherty blamed the critics, who 'did not possess sufficient blood to contract syphilis'.[31]

As a full-time professional writer with an extraordinarily keen sense of the market (he was even selling manuscripts of his short stories to collectors from very early on), O'Flaherty found himself in a quandary. Where to turn? Very deliberately he planned his next book, *The Informer*, as a serial and for film.[32] In the course of composition, the protagonist Gypo, 'a regular monster' – monster is a recurring O'Flaherty epithet for Gypo – grew on him. He felt sure the novel 'would make a good German film'.[33] To his chagrin and against his advice, his publisher, Jonathan Cape, issued the novel 'as a literary book and not a sensational one'.[34] O'Flaherty could all too easily imagine the unfortunate financial consequences for himself of this upgrading of his book from pulp fiction to literature. He wrote a bitter parodic review of the book to Garnett: 'It's a pity that Mr O'Flaherty can't give us something as good as *B. Soul*, none of the beauty, the high moral tone, the chaste simplicity of that remarkable book are visible in *The Informer*; sales = 747 copies'.[35] Thereafter his views on the novel fluctuated; by and large he seems to have succumbed to Cape's publicity, except for one vehement outburst in the pages of *Shame the Devil* where he described *The Informer* as the product of 'a calculated scheme for making money out of writing':

> Its publication proved that I was right. The literary critics, almost to a man, hailed it as a brilliant piece of work and talked pompously about having at last been given inside knowledge of the Irish revolution and the secret organization that had brought it about. This amused me intensely, as whatever 'facts' were used in the book were taken from happenings in a Saxon town during the sporadic Communist insurrection of about nineteen twenty-two or three. My trick had succeeded and those who had paid little attention to my previous work, much of it vastly superior, from the point of view of literature, to *The Informer*, now hailed me as a writer of considerable importance.[36]

The reference to 'happenings in a Saxon town' and the implied remoteness of whatever took place there to anything going on in Ireland is intriguing. O'Flaherty is covering his tracks. Before leaving for London he was on the editorial committee of the *Workers' Republic*, which, like radical newspapers all over the world in the 1920s, took an intense interest in the advance of communism on the Continent. Over several issues the paper reprinted a lengthy analysis of 'The Crisis in Germany' from the *Communist Review*. In introducing the analysis the 'Editorial Committee' made the point that the workers and small farmers of Ireland were following the same unfortunate trajectory as their counterparts in Germany. They were placing their trust in parliamentary Labour politicians, whereas only a complete social revolution would overthrow capitalism. This was the Comintern line at the time and the CPI followed it slavishly – just as it would change tack when Moscow decreed the opposite. The Editorial Committee concluded: 'We in Ireland are entering upon a period of development which in Germany is near its end.'[37] The almost typological habit of mind displayed here is quintessential O'Flaherty. If Elizabethan England was exemplary in the literary sphere, then Weimar was the place to watch politically.

And cinematically. Following the publication of *The Informer*, O'Flaherty pushed for a German translation of the book as his best hope of having it filmed. The novel was serialized in the *Frankfurt Zeitung*, and the first film rights were indeed sold in Germany, though the film was not to be made there. The earlier speculation that the novel 'would make a good German film' was again based on an accurate evaluation of the market. Germany, despite the attrition of war indemnities, was the leading film producer in Europe and the only country that posed any challenge to the near monopoly of Hollywood.

The extrinsic evidence points to O'Flaherty's interest, from the very beginning, in the cinematic possibilities of his narrative. His retrospective account in *Shame the Devil* is even more explicit. He wanted to write 'a sort of high-brow detective story':

> . . . its style [should be] based on the technique of the cinema.
> It should have all the appearance of a realistic novel and yet
> the material should have hardly any connexion with real life.
> I would treat my readers as a mob orator treats his audience
> and toy with their emotions, making them finally pity a
> character whom they began by considering a monster.[38]

How is this cinematic interest carried through in the novel itself? Hardly at all, in terms of the assimilation of such filmic techniques associated with high art narrative as montage, ellipsis or time lapse.

There is an additional problem. *The Informer* is written in a style that shifts disconcertingly between traditional nineteenth-century modes of telling and more modernist modes of showing. An intrusive narrator leaps out at us with such trite explanatory remarks as this on Gypo's fighting spirit: 'It was the savage joy that is always present in the Irish soul in time of danger, the great fighting spirit of our race, born of the mists and the mountains and the gurgling torrents and the endless clamour of the sea.'[39]

At a more pedestrian level, however, the novel is pervasively cinematic and overwhelmingly the product of an intensely visual rather than aural imagination. The 'dumb eye' of the camera that registers everything within its field of vision is everywhere present, as is a very disconcerting cinematic fragmentation of that field. So much is this the case that it would be tedious to work through *The Informer* picking out every instance where O'Flaherty finds a literary equivalent to a cinematic visual perspective or camera movement. From the opening tracking shot that takes us through the Dunboy Lodging House – where Frankie McPhillip becomes the 'lens' through which we view the house's interior – to the splendidly visualized action sequence of the last chapter given in long shot and grotesque close-up, we cannot but be aware of cinematic precedent. One passage can stand for many:

> The two of them stood in front of a window through which lamp-light was streaming, across Gypo's chest on to Mulholland's face. Mulholland's yellow face looked almost black in the lamp-light. It was furrowed vertically from the temples to the jaws with deep black furrows. The mouth was large and open, fixed in a perpetual grin that had absolutely no merriment in it, that fixed grin of sardonic contempt that is nearly always seen on the faces of men who make a business of concealing their thoughts. The nose was long and narrow. The ears were large. The forehead was

> furrowed horizontally. The skin on the forehead was very
> white in contrast to the dark skin on the cheeks. The furrows
> on the forehead were very shallow and narrow, like thin lines
> drawn with a sharp pencil. In fact, the whole appearance of
> the face was that of an artificial face, such as that produced
> in the dressing room of an actor by means of paints, etc.[40]

Positioning actors before an illuminated window was, of course, one of the classic methods of shooting a night sequence in the silent era. Here the oblique fall of the light across Gypo's chest serves to narrow the angle of vision on the face of his companion. The camera moves from a medium shot to close-up to a tight crawl up the unfortunate Mulholland's visage where, after an authorial intrusion, we get a series of discontinuous shots of ears, nose, etc., each boxed off in a separate sentence. The jerky repercussion of these visualized fragments (a literary analogue perhaps to the stop-motion camera) is what gives the passage its odd effect. And that effect would surely be risible were it not for the dour import of the narrator's comments. It may be one reason why he feels obliged to intervene so often in the novel, to restrain a method of description which mechanizes human behaviour in the direction of a Bergsonian version of the comic. Finally, we pull back to get a view of the whole ensemble, likened to the face of an actor coated with greasepaint (to push matters only a little, the 'etc.' with which the last sentence concludes presumably refers to the powder that was necessary to hide the glazed look of greasepaint under artificial light).

One of the many difficulties in the way of the literature–film comparison is that the cinema in question is often vague and idealized: it is frequently impossible to specify what particular films an author may have seen or wished to emulate. Bearing in mind our earlier caution with regard to the cinematographic novel (see the remarks on *Silhouettes* above), it is possible to hazard the opinion that O'Flaherty was influenced by silent German expressionism. Take the following, not untypical, passages from the novel:

His huge body, monstrous with strange movements, stood under the glare of the lamp that hung from the ceiling. His face, staring steadily at the woman, changed again and again, in response to the dark and mysterious suggestions that chased one another through his mind. At one moment his chest would heave and his limbs would stiffen. Then his breath would come with a snap. His jaws would set. His eyes would expand. A movement would begin in his throat. Then a sound like a curtailed shout would come from his nostrils.

He looked at Mulholland in amazement. His forehead wrinkled. His nostrils expanded and contracted. His thick lips moved backward and forwards, up and down. His face and his cropped skull shone in the light of the paraffin lamp that rested on the mantelpiece over the fire. The light also shone across his body, over a bulging bare shoulder, that stood out white and massive and round below his neck.[41]

The 'lighting' of these passages with their thick shadows and murky depths, the deliberate distortions and the crude, almost involuntary, movements of facial features and bodily limbs in response to vaguely apprehended inner seizures are typically expressionistic. Very extreme bodily reactions are described throughout the novel. Repeatedly Gypo grimaces, stares wide-eyed, flares his nostrils, sets his jaw, clutches his hands, stiffens his limbs, heaves his chest, all in the extravagant histrionic style of both the early biograph films and of German expressionism. This determined effort to portray strong emotion by means of rather gross, heavily stressed 'non-verbal' gestures in a supposedly realistic fiction is one of the main indicators of the novel's debt, not just to the silent cinema, but through it to popular melodrama. A real giveaway in this regard is the regularity with which Gypo follows a rule of the Delsarte school of acting which states that gesture must always precede verbal expression: only thus is the spoken word justified. (François Delsarte codified a system of melodramatic acting in the nineteenth century which found its way into the silent cinema.)

The expressionist film context we are proposing for the novel may help to explain some further puzzling features – *The Informer*'s lack of interest in psychology, for example. Gypo Nolan and Commandant Dan Gallagher are opposed as body and mind, brute instinct and sharp intelligence. They are embodied principles rather than characters endowed with credible psychological motives in a way that is quite commonplace in Weimar films of the 1920s. Like the so-called 'Revolutionary Organization' to which they are affiliated, they are abstractions.

There is even what is sometimes called an 'expressionist object' (e.g. an umbrella, sword or scarf intertwined with a character's fate) in the novel. This is Gypo's 'little tattered round slouch hat', which he alternately perches on his skull, twists nervously in his hands or stuffs in his pocket. When he temporarily mislays it, he feels bereft and anxious. When he expires on the last page, the hat rolls off.

Hats, of course, were everyday accoutrements of the silent era, as we recall from Charlie Chaplin films in particular (Beckett would later employ them with great dexterity in his plays and novels). But Gypo's slouch hat has a darker significance. He clings to it as a drowning man clings to a straw to ward off the dangers that threaten to emerge at any moment. The pathos of this hulking figure holding on at all costs to his tiny hat is one of the ways in which O'Flaherty evokes the reader's sympathy for Gypo. *We* may psychologize, even if the novel refuses to. The hat finds its origin in Winnicott's 'transitional object' – the tattered toy or blanket treasured by infants to protect them from breakdown in the absence of the mother. The clinging impulse may persist into disturbed adulthood (the 'ocnophile object').[42] Although Gypo, because of his great size and strength, is associated in the novel with a tree, a bull, a bear, our abiding impression of him is that, at bottom, he is a child.

Plate 5.   Die Strasse *(dir. Karl Grune, 1923).*

In proposing some of the ways in which O'Flaherty's narrative may have drawn on the very prestigious German cinema of the day, we can go a little further and suggest that he is influenced in particular by the *Kammerspielfilme* ('chamber-play film'). In these the protagonist is an anti-hero from the working or lower-middle class who is overwhelmed by the urban environment and ends his days by murder or suicide. The city is hellish, a place of violence, corruption and moral degradation and it is the street-by-night which brings out the infernal elements. A sub-group, known as 'the street film', of which Karl Grune's *Die Strasse* is the classic example, may be most pertinent here. It is important, however, to notice at least one striking difference between the narrative pattern of, say, *Die Strasse* and O'Flaherty's *Informer*. In the German film there are two worlds: the comfortable, boring home and the alluring, dangerous street. The protagonist moves from one to the other and back again. In O'Flaherty's novel there is no home, as it were, and everything takes place on the night street or its surrogates: the pub, the brothel, the fish-and-chip shop, the doss house, the ruined hideout. It is part of the extreme bleakness of O'Flaherty's vision that home is a distant, unreachable pastoral memory. It is also telling that, after traversing a series of increasingly sordid, secular locations, the novel should end in the sacred precincts of a church where a priest is saying mass. That is an important part of the so-called 'melodramatic excess' to which we must now briefly turn.

Melodramatic Excess?

The extraordinary upsurge of scholarly interest in melodrama has inspired a number of re-evaluations of figures as various as Balzac, Dostoevsky and Henry James. It has also had a major impact on film studies, where melodrama is increasingly regarded as the generic root of both Hollywood and German expressionist cinema.[43] The insights gained need to be broadened to encompass whole cultural traditions, such as, for example, the popular literature of the Irish late nineteenth and early twentieth century to which O'Flaherty's novels are an important contribution.

There is at least a prima-facie case to be made that melodrama is the relevant mode of political discourse for people caught up in a colonial or quasi-colonial situation. A strongly felt opposition between oppressor and oppressed, a monopathy of blame where all evil is external, and a pervasive reduction and stereotyping of human relations to a triangular pattern of victim, villain and liberator are but some of the indicators of this cast of mind. (It is the task of later historians, writers and intellectuals to dismantle such overdetermined simplifications.) Any dramaturgic or narrative practice where the action is set within a universe polarized between the powerful and the powerless is likely to lead to melodramatic presentation, as is evidenced in the work of the contemporary radical dramatists John Arden and Margaretta D'Arcy (*The Island of the Mighty*, *The Ballygombeen Bequest*).

Two forms of political melodrama, whether in the theatre or in other forms of discourse (ballad, popular history, romance), tend to dominate in a polarized world: the melodrama of triumph and the melodrama of protest.[44] The first was particularly difficult to manage in Ireland, because of a long history of defeats and disasters stretching from 1798 to the Great Famine. Writers circumvented the problem in much the same way as Irish sports journalists today handle the international defeats of the Irish soccer team: every failure becomes a moral victory. For a populace imbued with a pivotal sense of grievance, the melodrama of protest posed no problems.

What happens within a melodramatic tradition when failure is plain to see and the writer is determined to face up to it? This is exactly O'Flaherty's position in 1925. He writes *The Informer* in the shadow of a double defeat: the failure of the IRA to deliver a united Ireland and the failure of the CPI to have the slightest impact on the social and economic structures of the Free State. Counter-revolution has triumphed. Given his radical commitments and his romantic-realist proclivities in literature, O'Flaherty can only write a black melodrama of defeat. The hard-realist, relentless aspect of his strategy in the novel is to stage a conflict, not between capitalized Oppressor and Oppressed, but within the lower-case world of the oppressed themselves, a struggle to the death between a half-baked intellectual and 'the peculiar type of hog mind that constitutes an Irish peasant'. The Romantic traditions to which he was heir ensured that this conflict too would be couched in exalted, abruptly dualistic terms. He signalled his intention plainly to an Irish reader of the time by titling the novel *The Informer*, that generic villain of over a century of popular execration in ballad, memoir and popular theatre. Nothing, perhaps, better typifies the sea change in attitudes that has occurred today than the way in which contemporary informers have become, in that section of Ireland tutored by Conor Cruise O'Brien, figures of integrity and public spiritedness.

The daunting task the author set himself can be gauged from another, related consideration that will aid us to characterize more precisely the formal aspects of black melodrama. In *The Informer* we have a putative plot in which an unsympathetic protagonist suffers deserved misfortune – a plot form, incidentally, that held a special appeal for Jacobean writers. What O'Flaherty engaged to do was to win our sympathy for his repellent hero. There is a very full statement of his intentions in a letter to Garnett which shows how completely what the Russian Formalists called 'the emotional teleology of melodrama'[45] conditioned the style of the book. For the dominant of melodrama, its primary characteristic, is its method of playing on the emotions. Here is O'Flaherty *in extenso*:

I have envisaged a brutal, immensely strong, stupid character, a man built by nature to be a tool for evil-minded intelligence. The style is brutal at that stage, without finesse, without deviation, without any sweetness, short and curt like a police report. Then as other characters appear on the scene the character of the man changes gradually. Elements of cunning, of fear, of struggle that is born of thought, appear in him. The style changes to suit this, almost imperceptibly. More and more characters appear. The character is no longer brutal. Sympathy veers round and stands in the balance, for him or against him. He is now a soul in torment, struggling with evil influences. At this point the style becomes definitely sympathetic, lengthens itself out, softens, strikes a note of joy in the eternity of nature. Scenes of horror and sin present themselves.

Then with gathering speed the Informer is enmeshed by his enemies. His vast strength crumbles up, overwhelmed by the gathering waves of inconquerable intelligence. He stands alone, without the guidance of a mind to succour him, seeking an outlet for his useless strength, finding that it is no longer strength but a helpless thing, a target for the beings that press around to harass it. Intelligence, evil intelligence, is dominant and supreme, civilization conquers the first beginnings of man upwards.

Then the Informer makes a last effort to escape. Here the style completely changes and becomes like a wild storm, cascading, abandoned, poetic. From there it rises rapidly to a climax at this point:

'Shapeless figures dancing on tremendous stilts, on the brink of an abyss to the sound of rocks being tumbled below, in the darkness, everything without shape or meaning, gloom and preponderance, yawning, yawning abysses full of frozen fog, cliffs gliding away when touched leaving no foundation, an endless wandering through space, through screaming winds . . . crash.'

After that I strike a note of pity and finish on it. This is what I have tried to do.[46]

Clearly the Informer's dividedness is not that of a tragic hero, for the forces he struggles with are all outside of himself. So too the changes that occur within the novel are not a product of action or character but of the increasingly indulgent attitude of the narrator to Gypo Nolan and his deepening distaste for Commandant Dan Gallagher. While it is true that they stand in relation to one another as figures of instinct and intelligence (as O'Flaherty indicates), they are also opposed as Hardman and Gunman, a relation perfectly captured in the still from Ford's film where a stylish, trench-coated and armed Gallagher towers over a recumbent, dishevelled Gypo. It is not just Gallagher's intelligence that renders the hard-fighting, hard-drinking Gypo redundant, it is first of all the gun concealed in his erstwhile commander's pocket. O'Flaherty's tenderness for Gypo has been echoed in recent years by the lament for the passing of local hardmen in strife-torn Belfast and their replacement by paramilitary gunmen.

Hardmen (the condition often ran in families) were local heroes whose whole endeavour was to keep their reputations for ferocious drinking, whoring and fierce fist-fighting alive in their areas. They had an instinctive recognition that one enters folklore, not by being quiet and decent, but by being wild and dangerous. Once guns entered the equation, however, their traditional dominance of the streets came to an end and with it a colourful and bizarrely humane form of masculine assertion – at least in comparison to the faceless, balaclava-clad display of the paramilitaries. One old woman in *The Informer* recognizes Gypo for what he is:

> 'I wish I had a son like ye. Me own Jimmy, Lord have Mercy on him, was killed in the big war. He was the boy that could bate the polis! Don't be talkin'. I seen him wan night an' it took six o' them to pull him off a coal-cart an' he holdin' on to the horse's reins all the time with wan hand while he was fightin' them with th' other.'[47]

Inarticulate except for his fists, Gypo is one of the many mute figures who populate the world of melodrama, their very wordlessness to be read as a token of a fundamental innocence and closeness to nature.

It is a commonplace of criticism that we should be wary of an author's statement of intent. The caution is warranted with regard to O'Flaherty's letter to Garnett. He presents his work, strategically, largely under its 'respectable' classical realist aspects: a single main character with other characters and events subordinated to his career, linear development to a climax, chronological progression and causal sequence. This is only half the story. The fragile surface tension of realism in the ostensibly single-focus novel is repeatedly ruptured by another structure. This is the dual-focus narrative of melodrama, where two centres of power (here Gypo and Gallagher) contend for dominance as versions of Good and Evil. We understand their relation and their meaning not so much through the forward movement of plot or action as by means of a series of parallels and contrasts. As Rick

Altman remarked apropos the American film musical: 'Whereas the traditional approach to narrative assumes that structure grows out of plot, the dual-focus structure derives from character.'[48] The novel is best construed, then, in terms of the paradigmatic relationship between two figures rather than any syntagmatic development.

The crux of disputes about the embedded melodrama of *The Informer* reaches a focus in discussion of the final episode of the book. Gypo Nolan, riddled with bullets, stumbles into the church where mass is being offered for Frankie McPhillip, the man he has betrayed. He approaches Frankie's mother and begs forgiveness:

> It was very dark. He swallowed the blood in his mouth and he cried out in a thick whisper:
>
> 'Mrs McPhillip, 'twas I informed on yer son Frankie. Forgive me. I'm dyin'.'
>
> 'I forgive ye,' she sighed in a sad, soft whisper. 'Ye didn't know what ye were doin'.'
>
> He shivered from head to foot and bowed his head. He felt a great mad rush of blood to his head. A great joy filled him. He became conscious of infinite things . . . He cried out in a loud voice:
>
> 'Frankie, yer mother has forgiven me.'
>
> Then with a gurgling sound he fell forward on his face. His hat rolled off. Blood gushed from his mouth. He stretched out his limbs in the shape of a cross. He shivered and lay still.[49]

This, in its use of blatant coincidence and its implicit appeal to the crucified Christ's prayer to the Father ('Father, forgive them for they know not what they do'), is surely 'excessive'? Donoghue is clear on the question: 'It is an exorbitance. There are traditions in literature capable of sustaining such sublimity, but O'Flaherty is not in touch with them.'[50] This in spite of his earlier, very full acknowledgement of what he calls the 'city melodrama' of *The Informer*.

Plate 6. Gypo Nolan and Mrs McPhillip (The Informer, *dir. John Ford, 1935*).

Notions of excess or exorbitance are only tenable with reference to some law or norm. It is surely the norms and values of classic realist fiction that are being appealed to in condemning the passage. *Per contra*, what comes to the surface at the end of *The Informer* is another logic, that of the embedded melodramatic mode, which, true to its own internal dynamic, pushes for full, even blatant, expression. Rather than think in terms of a generalized 'city melodrama' we should perhaps consider the possibility of a specifically Catholic form of the mode, one distinct from the dominant puritan-democratic American and English varieties.[51] Repentance, a holy and happy death, rather than the just reward in this life of oppressed virtue are the markers of this counter-reformation tradition. (A good example is John Ford's 1926 melodrama *3 Bad Men*, which ends with the ghosts of the three outlaws riding into the sunset, their arms outstretched in an image of Golgotha-on-horseback.) It is just this overwhelming drama of eternal salvation with which O'Flaherty is in touch and that authorizes the intensity with which *The Informer* ends.

Earlier, in the section on the historical relevance or otherwise of O'Flaherty's novel, we were reluctant to press the charge of inaccuracy too hard. The reasons for maintaining that reluctance become clearer if we now advert to the devious ways in which history may enter a melodramatic text. Rather than simply reflecting social reality, the really vital points of contact between the historical order and the text may be those occasions where the text struggles with, objectifies and displaces an element of the social sphere in order to bring it to representation within the text's own formal constraints.[52] If we stand far back from Gypo and the narrative of *The Informer*, we suddenly see that, as well as being a Judas figure, he is, more interestingly perhaps, a type of the sorcerer's apprentice, a 'monster' (O'Flaherty's word) who escapes the control of his master and runs amok. This figure of the fantastic was very common in silent German cinema (*The Golem*, the *Homunculus* series, etc.) and was a response, however displaced and reified, to a definite historical moment. Thomas Elsaesser explains the significance of the monster in the German context:

> What is at issue is first of all a lack, an absence, an imbalance of forces, which is being compensated by means that themselves turn out to be excessive, irrepressible, destructive. As such, it is a formal principle – an attempt at finding a system of equivalence or substitution (which fails) . . .[53]

He goes on to suggest that the sorcerer's apprentice became the favourite metaphor for the radicals-turned-conservatives of German Romanticism post-1820 and of the expressionists in the wake of the failed socialist uprising of 1919. The suggestion here is that something of the same dynamic is at work in O'Flaherty's novel, written as it was at a time of counter-revolution in Ireland. Both the author's political waverings and his creature Gypo's excesses find their significance within the kind of 'imbalance of forces' adverted to by Elsaesser.

Ford in Weimar

If O'Flaherty's Ireland and Weimar have some intriguing common-alities, there were much stronger, more palpable, thematic and stylistic links between expressionism and Hollywood cinema in the person of John Ford. He was even to use parts of the elaborate set from F. W. Murnau's film *Sunrise* (1927) in the making of his own German–American melodrama *Four Sons* (1928). The two young directors established something of a mutual admiration society.

After the artistic success of *The Last Laugh* (1924), Murnau was headhunted by William Fox and brought to Hollywood to inculcate the artistic values and techniques of Hollywood's only cinematic rival. Given a large budget and a free hand, the 'German genius' directed what is perhaps the most luminous of all silent films, the wonderful *Sunrise*, with George O'Brien and Janet Gaynor in the lead. The film brought together the sophisticated artistry of German expressionism and the populism of Hollywood melodrama in a way that was to prove exemplary for many. Murnau had hoped to tell his story

Plate 7.   Sunrise *(dir. F.W. Murnau, 1927)*.

entirely without the use of inter-titles, but they were included as a concession to American audiences. John Ford thought it the greatest motion picture ever produced. Thereafter Murnau joined D. W. Griffith as a major influence on Ford's work, and there is a discernible, if atypical, 'expressionist' group of Ford films which include *Four Sons* (1928), *Hangman's House* (1928), *The Informer* (1935), *Mary of Scotland* (1936), *The Long Voyage Home* (1940) and *The Fugitive* (1947). *The Informer* was by far the most successful of these and, given the mode in which the original novel was cast, it seemed almost fated to become a John Ford expressionist movie.

Ford's self-apprenticeship to Murnau was far more extensive than is generally realized. His grandson's memoir gives it the emphasis it deserves. Ford, accompanied by his wife, travelled to Germany to shoot background material for *Four Sons* and immediately headed for Berlin and the UFA studios:

> Welcoming them warmly, Murnau allowed John to examine artists' renderings and design sketches, and explained in depth the pre-production techniques of German expressionist cinema. Fascinated, John screened the films of the German Golden Age: Lubitsch's [*sic*] *The Cabinet of Doctor Caligari* [1919], Lang's *Destiny* [1921] and *Metropolis* [1926], Murnau's own *Nosferatu* [1922] and *The Last Laugh* [1924] – films that used design and lighting techniques of the greatest sophistication to translate their stories to the screen in purely visual terms. John studied them scene by scene, making mental notes on their techniques, their slow deliberate rhythms. Many of the lessons he learned in Berlin would become a vital part of his own visual style.[54]

Was he shown Arthur Robison's *Schatten?* It seems likely, in that the opening sequences of his next and last silent, *Hangman's House* (1928), captures the brooding melancholy of Robison's film.

This intellectually enquiring, eager-to-get-to-the-cutting-edge-of-his-art Ford is a very different creature from the caricature of Irishness that he liked to play to the world. Like Liam O'Flaherty, he seemed imbued with a notion that male Irishness consisted of hard drinking, hard fighting, extravagant lying and a virulent anti-intellectualism. Yet both men were well read, had travelled the world and indulged expensive cosmopolitan tastes. An earlier generation of Irishmen at home and abroad had shared in the enabling delusion that they were all sons of kings. Ford's and O'Flaherty's generation had a more factual notion of themselves as sons of peasants, but with this went an affected boorishness that often belied extraordinary intelligence and creativity.

While Ford studied the masterpieces of Weimar film in Berlin, his 'cousin' Liam O'Flaherty's novel *The Informer* had just come out in translation. In an office on George Wilhelmstrasse there would shortly be written a shooting script, based on the book, by the well-known scriptwriter Rolf E. Vanloo and the director Arthur Robison. Also, just as Murnau had been poached by the Americans in an effort to raise the prestige and the artistic values of Fox Studios, so Robison would be poached by the British for exactly the same reasons. With him went the script of *The Informer.*

3

ARTHUR ROBISON'S *INFORMER*

Hollywood in Elstree

Aficionados of 1920s film will recall, if indeed they recall it at all, the first feature based on *The Informer* as a half-sound mish-mash with some very inferior foreign acting talent. There is a video of this version in the Film Institute of Ireland, which has further strengthened the notion that this is all there is to Robison's directorial debut in England. However, in the archive of the British Film Institute in London lies a seldom-seen silent version of the film. It is a beautiful piece of work, as fine an example as one could wish to see of late silent cinema. Archivists in the know like to claim that it is far superior to Ford's later 1935 film, but that is hardly to compare like with like. For, if Robison had changed the names of the characters and made no mention of O'Flaherty's novel, he could scarcely be accused of plagiarism. Except perhaps for the last scene, where Gypo dies at the foot of the cross, the plot of his film, unlike Ford's, has little enough to do with the novel – though both carry over its general atmospheric murkiness. The explanation for the existence of these two versions and the virtual relegation of one of them to oblivion is to be sought in the history of British film subsequent to the Cinematograph Films Bill becoming law in December 1927 and, more particularly, in the production policy of British International Pictures (known to those who worked there as 'The Porridge Factory') at the advent of sound technology. BIP's leading director at the time was the young Alfred Hitchcock, then on a twelve-picture contract. His *Blackmail* (1929) was made in the same year and in the same studio as *The Informer* and came under similar pressures. *Blackmail* survives as a masterpiece of British cinema. *The Informer* is scarcely known. What happened?

British Acts of Parliament have a way of inaugurating epochs. So it was with the Cinematograph Films Bill, which stipulated that UK cinemas show twenty per cent of British films in their programmes. It led to an immediate expansion in home production, which took two directions: one was to rush through low-budget thrillers and melodramas, which became known as 'Quota Quickies'; the other was to mount prestige productions with foreign stars and directors. The newly named British International Pictures, under its dynamic Scots owner John Maxwell, proclaimed in both title and logo (a staunch figure of Britannia standing before a turning globe) its aspiration to pursue the holy grail of British cinema: to make pictures of *international* appeal. Maxwell rightly recognized that German success in the field derived in a large part from the cultivation of a rich mix of talents from many different nationalities and traditions (theatrical, pictorial, musical). While continuing to produce 'Quickies', he also emphasized the cosmopolitan approach and invited over a number of European and American directors, such as E. A. Dupont (*Moulin Rouge*, 1928), to work on his films at Elstree. The point of hiring such prestigious directors was to bring in their train international stars (and technicians), in the hope that Elstree films would penetrate overseas markets. Many established Continental directors had virtual stock companies who moved with them from project to project. Thus Robison brought to *The Informer* not only the Hungarian actress Lya De Putti, with whom he had worked on *Manon Lescaut* (1926), but also the much sought after Emil Jannings, from his days in Berlin. As it happened, Jannings could not be released in time from other commitments and the Swedish star Lars Hanson took over as male lead.

All of these actors were currently working in Hollywood, part of that first wave of an undifferentiated 'German invasion' that included Murnau. Their American careers were in deep trouble. With the advent of sound, guttural foreign accents were a definite liability: if they wanted to go on working in the Anglophone world they had to chase silent films wherever they were being made. Lya De Putti's star interview with *The Picturegoer* in April 1929 barely disguises a career in decline – despite announcing that she has brought her Packard car and private Avro Avian aeroplane with her for her London debut in *The Informer*.[55] But even in England the sound posse was catching up with her. In the same month as she gave the interview, two sound stages with RCA Photophone recording equipment were installed by British International Pictures and what is widely regarded as the first British 'all-talking' feature, Hitchcock's *Blackmail*, was in production. It would be shot as a silent and the sound added later. It worked. Not so the half-baked solution found to get Robison's film out of the studio and into the film palaces.

The shooting script for BIP's *The Informer* by Rolf E. Vanloo and Artur (*sic*) Robison, with dialogue by Benn Levy, must be one of the most intriguing documents in cinema history. It literally straddles the changeover from silent to sound as, quite startlingly, does the film itself. (Since there is no commercially available print or video available, a plot summary, of the kind that nobody reads, is to be found in the Appendix of this book.)

The first part of the script has silent inter-titles written on the left side of the page. Then, from Scene 313 (the 'interrogation' of Katie Fox), spoken dialogue is typed in red on the right-hand margin. Not inappropriately, perhaps, the first spoken sentence in a film of Irish reference goes: 'As a member of the Party, you will answer a few questions.'[56] It comes as quite a shock, when watching the film for the first time, to hear the English actor Warwick Ward (Dan Gallagher) suddenly break into speech halfway through and pronounce the recommissioned Captain Gallagher's words in a chiselled Knightsbridge accent. Those in the original audience who knew from the pages of *The Picturegoer* that leading lady Lya De Putti (Katie Fox) hardly spoke English must have been equally startled to hear her dainty, dubbed, upper-class tones. So too with the Swedish actor Lars Hanson as Gypo Nolan: his lugubrious, dubbed received pronunciation, applied with a trowel, is greatly at variance with his working-class docker role. The technicians at Elstree Studios had more than a few questions to answer as they struggled with the new technology. Unlike Hitchcock's *Blackmail* (the ear-arresting 'knife sequence' in particular), nothing can be made of sound here as a signifying code in an artistic sense.

The halfway-through dubbing is simply awful. Moreover, not all the elements of the rich hybridity promised by an Irish novel, a German-American director, an international cast of actors and an English production company came to fruition. The masterful silent version, intended as a prestige project but now redundant with the advent of sound, was rapidly buried and forgotten in the rush to issue a 'Quota Quickie' for the newly equipped talkie cinemas. It did, however, receive a positive notice in the snobbish-about-sound journal *Close Up*. (*Close Up*, unlike *The Picturegoer*, catered for the emerging art-house and the more sophisticated end of the industry.) Intriguingly, the review gives the silent film under both an English and German title – *The Informer / Die Nacht nach dem Verrat* ('*The Night after the Betrayal*') – and claims 'it proves at least that a good film can come out of a British studio through a British censor, and it is difficult to understand why the patriots did not give it a bit more boosting, because it fully deserves it'. Praise is tempered by a reservation that the film wasn't given the Russian treatment: 'this story of the Irish rebellion is so eminently suitable for treatment *à la russe* that it becomes almost a duty to lament over what might have been'. Nevertheless, 'lighting and technique stamp the picture as the work of the Director of *Schatten*, *Manon Lescaut* and *Looping the Loop* [1928]'.[57] This is a pointer to a consideration that will only be fully theorized some seventy years later in the work of Thomas Elsaesser, the notion that cinema style, especially German expressionism, is perhaps a matter of design to enhance a product rather than some deep intrinsic expression of subject matter.

From internal evidence, it seems that the silent script was first written in German and was based very loosely on the recently published German translation of O'Flaherty's novel, *Die Nacht nach dem Verrat*. At one point in the manuscript there is a note explaining the phrase 'I blabbed on him': 'Translation note: *Verpfiffen* – "blow the gaff/blabbed/squeaked/narked"',[58] which suggests that the writer was working from the German. The typescript now in the archive of the Film Institute of Ireland is probably a make-over of a script originally intended for the UFA studios in Berlin.

It is impossible to tell exactly, at this distance in time and on the evidence available, who was responsible for what. Robison is often given the sole writing credit, though Ralph E. Vanloo is given first credit in the manuscript. There is also the intrusive hand of 'script-doctor' Benn Levy in the second spoken part of the typescript. Levy was just beginning a career as a prolific playwright in London and New York (*This Woman Business, A Man With Red Hair*) and was brought in by the BFI to write the dialogue for both Hitchcock's *Blackmail* and Robison's *Informer*. As with similar movies in the early days of sound in Hollywood, the introduction of a playwright to handle dialogue proved less than fortunate. Speech in both films is stilted and stagy. There is a similar uncertainty surrounding the final edit of the film and the degree to which Robison was involved. Was the film botched by an insensitive Elstree editor, as Paul Rotha suggests,[59] or did Robison have a say? The deliberate (and very German expressionist) way in which one scene or sequence takes place in the shadow of another suggests to this viewer that he had. As early as 1930 Paul Rotha wrote a damning indictment of the waste of people like Robison at Elstree:

> The importation of foreign talent did not have the same influence in British studios as it did at an earlier date in Hollywood. It will be remembered that the work of Lubitsch, Murnau, Pommer, and Seastrom had serious effect on the minds of the younger school of American directors. But in Britain, Arthur Robison, E. A. Dupont, and Henrik

Galeen, three directors of talent, have had no effect on the Elstree school. On the contrary, their ideas were totally misunderstood and unappreciated in our studios. Foreign directors failed to discover in Britain the collectivism and teamwork so vital to film production. They were unable to understand our ideas of picture-sense and we were at a loss to interpret their filmic outlook.[60]

This judgement has stood the test of time. Perhaps the best way to approach Robison's *Informer* is to view it not as a British, or indeed 'Irish', film at all, but as a late outrider of Weimar expressionism foundering in the 'porridge factory' of Elstree.

Dr Arthur Robison

Arthur Robison is one of the most elusive and least discussed of major directors. Perhaps the fact that he was born in Chicago in 1888 of German-American-Jewish parentage and worked in Germany, France, England, America and Austria accounts for his absence from many of the standard handbooks and guides, which prefer less peripatetic, more nationally contained, careers. Like many of those involved in the early years of cinema, he came to the industry from outside and with an invaluable range of non-cinematic experience. Though born and brought up in the States, he trained as a doctor at the University of Munich but quickly abandoned a medical career in favour of journalism and acting in Switzerland. In 1914, at the age of twenty-six, he moved to Berlin and entered the burgeoning German film industry as a scriptwriter. His directorial debut took place two years later with the horror film *Nächte des Grauens*. It was a remarkable beginning, if only because of the big-name actors involved – Werner Krauss and Emil Jannings among them. Six years later in 1922 Robison directed his second feature, *Schatten*. It would earn him a permanent place in the history of cinema and is one of the most beautiful – and puzzling – products of

51

the great age of German expressionism. It is the only one of his sixteen films to receive the accolade of an extended write-up (by the Irish critic and archivist Liam O'Leary) in the current English-language bible of film, the *International Dictionary of Films and Filmmakers*.[61]

Six silent German films followed *Schatten*. The more successful were *Manon Lescault*, made in 1926 with Lya De Putti as leading lady (Marlene Dietrich had a small supporting role), and the following year a very popular and commercially innovative UFA/Paramount co-production of *Der Letzte Walzer* ('*The Last Waltz*') with Willy Fritsch. By 1929, just before the call came from London to direct *The Informer*, Dr Robison, as he was known, had a reputation for successful costume drama and for his ability to work not only with the leading European actors and actresses but with such brilliant technical staff as cameraman Fritz Arno Wagner and set designer Paul Leni. He also had a reputation as a 'hands-on' director who concerned himself with every aspect of filmmaking, including the script. Hardly surprising, then, that the nascent British film industry, casting around to recruit new talent and German expertise, fastened on Robison.

There is a telling parallel between Robison's progress (if progress it is) from *Schatten* to *The Informer* and F. W. Murnau's development from *Nosferatu* (1922) to *Sunrise* (1927). Both *Schatten* and *Nosferatu* were, as it were, one hundred per cent proof German expressionism. *The Informer* and *Sunrise*, made outside Germany, were cast in more subdued stylistic idioms, closer to mainstream classical realism as it was developing in Hollywood. Nevertheless, both films contain bravura passages employing expressionist *mise-en-scène* as if to demonstrate what could be achieved: in *Sunrise* the haunting moonlit sequence on the moors where the Man meets the City Woman; in *The Informer* the topos of the night chase over dipping roofs and between clustered, sculptural chimneys. There is a sense in both films too of the camera delighting in its own freedom of movement, as when it surges out from constricted interiors and static situations to follow the protagonists into the bustle and urgency of the city.

An interesting case can be made on the back of this overt indulgence in expressionist technique. It is to the effect that, far from being the atavistic voice of a reawakened German Romanticism or the precursory vision of Nazi totalitarianism, expressionism in German film was a calculated response to the market. Post-World War I, German exports to the rest of Europe and America were having a hard time. Quite unexpectedly, *Caligari* became a great international hit. It made economic sense to apply the successful formula (chiaroscuro lighting, stylized sets, histrionic acting) to other 'products' designed to woo hostile foreign audiences. Hence the creation in expressionist film of a 'German imaginary' for export.[62]

There is, it has to be said, something woefully reductive about strong versions of the economist argument. It is reminiscent of similar, disenchanted approaches to yet another manifestation of European Romanticism, the Celtic Twilight, as the meretricious fabrication of an Irish imaginary for export to Britain. The magic of the Wind Among the Reeds or of the Haunted Screens of Weimar cannot, finally, be accounted for in solely pragmatic terms. It is nonetheless the case that there is a marked shift away from the high expressionist mode, especially with regard to the attempt to cinematically represent subjective states, in the work of Robison and Murnau once they were free of Germany.

In the case of Robison, what was most evidently abandoned, at least in comparison to his earlier work, was exuberant externality of style. His encounter, as a Continental director, with the British film industry was everything he might have expected it to be. From the time of Chaucer's domestication of adulterous French *amour courtois* into glad marital affection, the English have had a genius for taking the wilder impulses of Continentals, lowering the voltage and making them more humanly tolerable. (The way in which the high-octane visionary work of the contemporary Austrian seer Rudolf Steiner was made intelligible – and wonderfully stimulating – in the philology of Owen Barfield is yet another example.) Suffice it to note that, as Paul Rotha points out, there is no such thing as a British school of expressionist cinema, despite the presence in some numbers of German directors and technicians in the late 1920s and early 1930s. Nevertheless, Robison's almost total recasting of *The Informer* to give a central role to Katie Fox and the atmosphere of surveillance that pervades the piece make it, to all intents and purposes, a Weimar film shorn of stylistic extravagance.

Robison made only the most perfunctory gestures towards establishing an Irish ethos for his work. There is – what else? – a bottle of Guinness stout on the table, a map of Ireland on the wall of Party Headquarters and, wonderful to behold, a Garda Síochána Foot and Mouth poster in the police station. But the police (unlike the Gardaí), and indeed almost everybody else in sight, are armed to the teeth and, despite the brief appearance of carriages from the London and North-Eastern Railway, the atmosphere and general decor suggest Berlin, which was just then rejoicing in the title 'murder capital of Europe'. *Lustmord,* or sexual murder, was an obsession of the German popular press of the day and it is in this direction, rather than Irish politics, that Vanloo and Robison forced their rewrite of O'Flaherty's novel. The impression that this is a German city rather than a half-hearted Dublin is strengthened by reference to the script – a lengthy slapstick chase sequence (dropped from the film) takes place in a dance cabaret utterly unlike anything to be found off O'Connell Street. Most interesting of all is the way Robison gives Katie a central role in the drama. She is the German *die newe frau* incarnate. The action revolves around a series of misunderstandings and false assumptions concerning her which lead to the shooting dead of her lover.

One of the most fundamental decisions a writer or adaptor must make with regard to the material he or she deals with is whether to treat it extensively or intensively. The first spreads the action over a lengthy period of time and many locales with interwoven sub-plots; the second focuses on the last crucial hours of an action, has fewer locales and involves a small group of people. O'Flaherty's *Informer* is clearly written in the intensive mode, with its single action taking up a mere twelve hours. Robison recasts it in a more extensive format, in which the remote trigger of events – McPhillip's act of murder – is shown rather than recalled in flashback. He does so in order to accommodate the crucial change he wants to make: in his film, events are to be precipitated by Katie Fox.

In the opening sequence at Party Headquarters, Katie is attached to a fresh-faced Francis McPhillip and rebuffs an advance by Gypo Nolan. Shortly thereafter, when Francis goes on the run after shooting the Chief of Police (the script has the 'Lord Mayor'), she switches her affections to Gypo. Some time is required for Gypo and Katie to build the kind of passionate relationship that will sustain the subsequent action. Hence the inclusion as action of what is given in flashback in the novel. Robison manages the time lapse in a wonderfully economic two-shot sequence. In the first, we see the back of McPhillip's head as he makes for the mountains. In the second, he turns to the camera and his face, now bearded and gaunt, tells its own story of suffering and loss. He skulks back to the city to say farewell to Katie before leaving for America. It is at this point that Gypo grows suspicious that Katie is about to go off with her former lover. To prevent that happening, he betrays McPhillip to the police. Thus the whole motivation for the plot has been changed to one of jealous love based on misunderstanding – we are later to learn that Gypo's suspicions were unfounded. One of the many symmetries of the film plot is that Katie will in turn betray Gypo as a result of her own misapprehension of his motives.

To carry off the role of *femme fatale*, the character of Katie Fox is radically altered from the pathetic drink-and-drug-sodden creature of O'Flaherty's novel. As played by the enchanting Lya De Putti, she is the Weimar vamp personified – seductive, sexually liberated, the equal of any man. (The script, lamely, attempts to naturalize these virtues by repeated reference to Katie having an Irish temperament which will never bear injustice.) When we first see her she is the solitary female at a meeting of the Party and a recurring tableau in the film has a white, flower-faced Katie as the focus point of a group of dark-clothed men. When trouble irrupts, as it does in the first minute of the film, it is Katie who breaks out the guns and helps to load them for her beleaguered comrades. Later, when she is interrogated at a Party inquiry about her relationship to Gypo, she frankly admits that he is her lover. Under pressure because of the mounting evidence against him, she can even deliberately *perform* her vampishness to buy Gypo time. It is worth quoting the original script at this point to give a flavour of the acting style required. Katie indulges in a contrived outburst in response to Gallagher's order that the informer be captured alive:

> KATIE *is standing up with closed eyes. She stands for a moment, swaying a little with the strength and violence of her feelings. Then she opens her eyes; with her mouth drawn into a thin line she says (Mr Levy suggests that she says this with great fire):*
>
> KATIE: He's to be brought here alive, is he? Why alive? Are you afraid to plug him like the dirty rat he is? (*Scornfully.*) Call yourselves men? And you treat an informer like a bad boy at a Sunday School. He was my lover; my lover, I say, and I don't care who knows it. But my lover was Gypo, the brave comrade. Not Gypo the Informer.[63]

The very mention of a bad boy at a Sunday school shows how remote the film is from any attempt to recreate the milieu of the original novel. The word 'comrade' too is curious. Are there leftist connotations? The internecine warfare between the Party and the never specified Opposition portrayed in the film, the Frei-Corps-officer demeanour of Captain Gallagher who seems to be on reasonably good terms with the police, all suggest that the Party is rather of the reactionary right, perhaps even National Socialist. Paul Rotha's rueful remark regarding visiting German directors – 'We were at a loss to interpret their filmic outlook' – is nowhere more evident than in the indeterminacy of time and place introduced here by Levy's dialogue. Katie's idiom veers from American gangster ('plug him like a dirty rat!') to genteel English to German New Woman ('He was my lover . . . and I don't care who knows it'). Politics, however, are largely irrelevant to the story of the lovers' passion. Unusually, the vamp is not sacrificed to save the male lead and Gypo goes to his death, locking a door behind him so that Katie will not be caught in the final hail of gunfire.

It would be false to give the impression that Katie is treated in an entirely positive way in Robison's *Informer*. Whether it is her putative 'Irish temperament' or the conventional instability of the New Woman in films of the day, the main turning points hinge on her irrational outbursts. She precipitates the betrayal and death of her first lover, McPhillip, by falsely claiming that she intends going to America with him in order to hurt Gypo. In turn she betrays Gypo to the Party when Gallagher presents her with apparent evidence that Gypo has been involved with another woman. If one were unaware of the O'Flaherty novel, one might well consider that it is Katie who is the informer of Robison's title.

Apart from the foregrounding of Katie as a seductive vamp, the other Weimar-inspired element of the film is surely its pervasive sense of surveillance, a sense that everybody is being watched. (Two years on, Fritz Lang's *M* (1931) would give the theme its classic statement.) From the very beginning, Robison sets up a simple pattern of spatial relations that allows for surveillance to take place in the most economical way possible. Basically, the pattern is that one space watches another, adjoining space. Three early instances will exemplify how this works. In the opening sequence, the committee room at Party Headquarters (where Gallagher is trying to launch a new, non-violent policy) is suddenly vulnerable to armed assailants at the window of a room on the same level across the street. When the Opposition attack through the front door, the landing and stairwell of Headquarters are juxtaposed in a similar combative fashion. More complex, but still adhering to the same basic pattern, is the spatial arrangement of Katie's flat, where much of the important action takes place. Katie is a milliner who has three rooms: a parlour, a kitchen and a bedroom. (Her adequate accommodation undermines claims that the real reason the film was banned in Ireland was because of its savage portrayal of Dublin's slums.) In the scene where McPhillip returns from the hills to visit her one last time, Robison uses this space in the manner of farcical comedy, but to much darker purpose. There is a policeman patrolling the street outside. When Gypo arrives, Katie hides McPhillip in the kitchen while entertaining Gypo in the parlour. Thus the policeman is on the lookout for McPhillip; McPhillip is watchful of his rival Gypo in the next room; and Gypo observes McPhillip in a conveniently placed mirror.

Equally telling is the scene which follows, in which Katie goes to Mother McPhillip's shop and is tailed by Gypo. The shop has bulging leaded windows – the kind favoured by the expressionist camera – and the viewer is very forcefully placed in a voyeuristic position in the street looking into an illuminated room. Katie arrives and, in one of the film's emphatic gestures, looks behind her to see if she is being followed. Once inside the shop, she kisses McPhillip farewell. Cut to Gypo's eyes, dilated with jealousy, glowering in at them. Through a repeated pattern, then, of adjacent agonistic spaces and the use of fairly standard expressionist lighting techniques (quaking shadows, barred lights, the muslin curtain on Katie's door which both holds and distorts the silhouette), Robison established a fraught universe for his film that bears a strong family likeness to other paranoid portrayals of the city in Weimar cinema. In this regard, one of the great curiosities of the piece is his Hamletic direction of Lars Hanson as Gypo. This Gypo is utterly unlike O'Flaherty's hulking peasant or the later superb shambling performance by Victor McLaglen in the role.

Plate 8. The Informer *(dir. Arthur Robison, 1929).*

Though wearing a docker's peaked cap, he comes across as more of a *fin de siècle* bohemian or unemployed intellectual, an impression heightened by the kerchief worn round his neck. Hanson, because of his refined demeanour, had a reputation in Hollywood for playing weak-willed men (such as Dimmesdale in Seastrom's *The Scarlet Letter*, 1926) and priests. Robison went with the stereotype. Pointing to his heart as the gunmen beneath open fire, Gypo goes to his death, glad to be rid of a wearisome life.

The director pulls out all the expressionist stops for the informer's last agony in the church, with its guttering candles, arched windows and shadowy pews. There is here an intriguing possible subversion of the Catholic melodrama of the novel's end when Gypo approaches Frankie's mother for forgiveness. The only available print is difficult to interpret at this point, but she seems to stare back at him vacant-eyed and without recognition. The inter-title certainly grants him absolution ('May He forgive you as I do'). However, it is not at all clear from the visual evidence that this is actually what Robison intended. Gypo's final exultant stumble towards the crucifix, then, may be the last act of a deluded man who falls, not so much at the foot of the cross, as at the foot of the camera. Robison, as anybody who has seen *Schatten* will recognize, was quite capable of such self-referential effects.

The half-sound version received a lukewarm reception and quickly disappeared from British screens. Irish reviewers who reported home were scathing. Mary Manning wrote for the *Irish Statesman*: 'The cultural accents of Dublin's underworld, the cardboard inanities of the studio Dublin and the naivete of the captions were vastly entertaining. No Dubliner must miss this film.'[64] But Dubliners were not allowed to see it, by a censor who was ready to admit that he knew nothing about film but did know the Ten Commandments:

> This sordid show of Chicago gunmen, armed police, and prostitutes are shown at gunplay and soliciting in the standard slum of movieland. [*The Informer*] was offered as a realistic picture of the underworld of Dublin. It is a pity that the citizens cannot take action against the producers for a libel against our City. I refuse to grant a certificate for the exhibition of the impudent and mischievous distortion.[65]

This was progress of a kind. At least the censor was concerned with the good name of the city rather than the virtue of Irish peasants in the West.

4

THE FORD–NICHOLS *INFORMER*

....

An Absolute Masterpiece?

John Ford's *The Informer* (1935) became, in an oxymoron of the day, an 'instant classic'. It won four Academy Awards, for the director, for Victor McLaglen as Best Actor, Dudley Nichols for Best Screenplay and Max Steiner for Best Score. It was nominated for Best Picture of the Year but lost out to MGM's *Mutiny on the Bounty*. Dudley Nichols became the first person ever to turn down an Academy Award (see below). For four decades thereafter the film would regularly appear on lists of the 'Twelve Best Films' and it made Ford's name as a serious artist. Yet today, if we turn to the popular film guide *Time Out*, it is to read the following querulous remarks: 'What do critics dream about? John Ford got the best reviews of his career for this heavy-handed, humourless and patronising art film.'[66] What happened to *The Informer*'s once seemingly unassailable reputation? Better still: did it deserve its early canonization?

What happened is what Andrew Sarris calls 'aesthetic amnesia'.[67] The critics who hailed it as the first artistic breakthrough in American sound cinema had not only forgotten the earlier work of Sternberg and Lubitsch but, most culpably, German expressionism of the twenties. So cataclysmic and epoch-making had been the arrival of the talkie, it was as if nobody remembered Murnau's *Sunrise* of a mere six years earlier.

All artistic work declares itself by swerving away from the current artistic norm, and so with Ford's *Informer*. At a time of overwhelming verbosity in film, of words, words, words and of clear, well-lit objective images, he deviated sufficiently from the dominant codes to have his film instantly recognized as something new and

Plate 9. Victor McLaglan and Bette Davis, Best Actor and Actress, Oscar Ceremony, 1935. Reproduced courtesy of the Academy of Motion Pictures, Arts and Sciences.

compelling. As so often with innovation in the arts, Ford moved forward by moving backwards to adopt the style (perhaps the 'ornament' would be a better term) and aesthetic of an earlier decade and of another tradition. The move was not simply meretricious – the novel he chose to film certainly beckoned in a German expressionist direction and he made very good use of what he had learned from Murnau – but it is difficult today to see it as the completely innovative artistic statement it was once held to be. The quick, deflationary *Time Out* assessment, however, is not the only one in the field. Other popular film guides continue to award it three or four stars and in 1998 it came out on video in the 'Golden Classics' series. It has proved its classic credentials in the only way that really counts – the ability to stand the test of time.

Up to this point *The Informer* has been described as a Ford film, in accordance with the tyrannical convention that ascribes films solely to directors. However, there is evidence to suggest that *The Informer* is more properly a writer's film. In the manuscript library of Yale University there is a special copy of the mimeographed script of the RKO production presented to its author Dudley Nichols and autographed by John Ford and the cast. Nichols's script is extraordinarily precise as these things go. It is worth extensive quotation to demonstrate the sheer density of detail and the almost formulaic way in which 'expressionism' is applied. These are the opening shots:

EXT. DUBLIN STREET – EVENING

WIDE ANGLE SHOT *of a Dublin street corner. Thick fog. Somewhere in distance a street singer is singing to a fiddle. Before us is a blank brick wall where diverse bills are posted, some tattered some new, but all vaguely seen through the fog. A lamppost on the corner lights this wall and throws shadows up this side street. Around the corner past this lamppost is a brighter street – our Dublin street which extends for a short block past a fish and chip*

> *shop to the public house on the corner. It is in front of that pub that this lonely music is coming from. But all that is out of scene now. Out from the fog down this dark street emerges the slouching figure of* GYPO NOLAN. *Desolate and down and out. Hands shoved in pockets. An old felt hat on his head. An old white muffler wrapped round his throat. In this* FULL SHOT *we see him come out of the fog like some strange fish out of a mysterious ocean of mist. He halts near the corner and stares at a small poster about the height of his head, caught in the slanting light from the lamppost. Now* GYPO *is in the light as well as the poster and* CAMERA MOVES IN *to* CLOSE SHOT *of poster past* GYPO's *head. We see a picture of* FRANKIE McPHILLIP *(type of Wallace Ford) and read the lettering:* 20 POUNDS FOR INFORMATION.[68]

The script of the ninety-one-minute film continues in this same elaborate shot-by-shot fashion for two hundred pages. The rule of thumb goes that one page of script equals one minute of film. Here the extra pages are taken up with the most detailed shooting instructions, the whole thing cast in a pervasive foggy expressionist mode. While not wishing to suggest that, with this script in hand, all Ford had to do was shoot by numbers, it is legitimate to ask: whose film is this? Could it really be that Ford, as Tag Gallagher suggests, actually *dictated* the script to Nichols?[69] This suggestion seems to have originated in Dan Ford's memoir of his grandfather and to be part of a long-running effort to denigrate Nichols and elevate Ford (they worked on fourteen films together). Dan Ford's reconstruction of the writing process, some forty-seven years after the event is remarkably – and suspiciously – detailed:

> Dudley Nichols was first to bear the brunt of John's enthusiasm for *The Informer*. They worked on the script in the living room of John's Odin Street house, where John, dressed only in a bathrobe and chomping on endless cigars, dictated the script scene by scene. Nichols often found

himself standing up and shouting to make himself heard. John's typical response if they didn't agree was that Nichols didn't 'understand the Irish temperament' or that he had no 'first hand experience with the Irish people'. When that didn't work, John exploded in a tirade of personal insults, calling the writer a 'supercilious egghead' who wanted to write 'a doctoral dissertation on the origins of the Irish proletariat'. When they finally agreed on a scene, Nichols would write it down and John would go over it, making brutal cuts in Nichols's dialogue.

When the first draft was completed, Nichols typed it up and the whole process began again. Only after countless rewrites and the most intense effort did John consider the script ready. By then, Nichols was so exhausted from the work and from John's bullying that he vowed never to work for him again.[70]

The source of this heroic vignette of the *auteur* as Hollywood demiurge was presumably Ford himself.

Here is Dudley Nichols's account in a letter to Lindsay Anderson that is full of generous praise for Ford:

I had just completed the script for De Mille [Cecil B. De Mille's *The Crusades*, 1935], when Ford and a producer at RKO named Cliff Reid called me with enthusiasm. They had obtained approval to film *The Informer*, against much studio resistance . . . I wrote the script at white heat in a phenomenally short time and there was never another draft – the only script I can remember in which there were never any changes or revisions or further drafts. I had of course been mulling the story for a long time and gathering ideas on how to do it. I had a few talks with Ford beforehand but nothing specific was discussed. Then we had one fruitful session together with Max Steiner, who was to write the

> music, Van Nest Polglase who was to do the sets, Joe August
> was the cameraman, and a couple of technicians. This, to my
> mind, is the proper way to approach a film production – and
> it is, alas, the only time in 25 years I have known it to be
> done: a group discussion before a line of script is written.[71]

This was written in 1953. Fourteen years earlier and some four years
after *The Informer* was made, he had written to much the same effect
in the *National Board of Review Magazine*. Nichols was a firm believer
in film as a collaborative art and in his magazine piece he stressed the
necessity of common endeavour: 'We wanted to make something that
had integrity as a whole, not a picture that was written in one mood,
photographed in another, directed in another and would finally
emerge as just a Hollywood picture.'[72] This is virtually a definition of
what expressionism meant in the cinema of the day. He was even to
write on another occasion that 'Screenplays are not complete works
in themselves, they are blueprints of projected films'.[73]

   Who to believe? All the evidence stacks up in favour of the Dudley
Nichols version of events. And given everything we know about
Ford's pugnacious egoism it is extremely unlikely that he would have
inscribed a presentation copy of a script in honour of Nichols that he
himself had dictated. Nichols, unlike Ford, had a reputation for
veracity. On this score nothing better illustrates the difference
between the two men than their respective reaction to the award of
Oscars to *The Informer*. Nichols refused his award in a noble letter to
the Academy:

> To accept it would be to turn my back on nearly a thousand
> members of the Writers Guild, to desert those fellow-writers
> who ventured everything in the long-drawn-out fight for a
> genuine writers organization, to go back on convictions
> honestly arrived at, and to invalidate three years work in the
> Guild, which I should like to look back upon with self-
> respect . . .

> A writer who accepts an Academy Award tacitly supports the Academy, and I believe it to be the duty of every screenwriter to stand with his own, and to strengthen the Guild, because there is no other representative autonomous organization for writers which aims at justice for employer and employee alike, and which is concerned solely with the betterment of the writing craft.[74]

Ford at first refused his award in support of the Guild, but a few months later relented and quietly accepted the Oscar for Best Director. In the vicious, long-drawn-out war between the Academy (a company union) and the Guild there were, as in every war, informers, touts and turncoats aplenty. The acrid political atmosphere in Hollywood in 1935, with the growing paranoia about reds-under-the-bed, was not very different from that in O'Flaherty's novel. Perhaps that was one of the unspoken reasons why the action of *The Informer* was set back in time to the Irish War of Independence. The actual story of internecine struggle may have been a little close to the bone for a Hollywood that was at war with itself.

Nichols's script and Ford's direction raise, in an acute way, a problem touched on earlier: to what degree is expressionism in the cinema a matter of visual design analogous, say, to the application of stucco and ornate plaster foliage to brickwork? With regard to *The Informer*, at least, the answer seems clear enough. The solid structure, the bricks and mortar so to speak, is classical Hollywood narrative of which Nichols was both one of the earliest and best practitioners and theorists. The *clair-obscure* lighting is the externally applied 'poached' styling. A small, though telling, example of the way in which content follows form here is the use of expressionist atmosphere. There is the obligatory fog suffusing and dimming all the exterior scenes. At the same time and in the same frames a 'wanted' poster (an 'expressionist object' *par excellence*) is blown by the wind through the streets. It moves around like a poltergeist, clinging to the legs of the guilty Gypo. Fog and strong gusting winds do not occur together in nature. Ford's editing is so seamless that the viewer is scarcely aware of the subterfuge.

Nichols, in his occasional discursive notes on scenario writing, advanced a few clear principles in the belief that 'it is the writer who has matured the film medium more than anyone else in Hollywood'.[75] Chief among them was the command to write as a camera and thereby avoid the talkativeness of the theatre. A second principle held that, if the stage was the medium of action, then the screen was the medium of reaction: 'It is through identification with the person *acted upon* on the screen and not with the person acting, that the film builds up its oscillating power with an audience.'[76] Conflict was central to both media, but it was to this second character that the camera instinctively roves. Nichols's actual screenwriting practice yielded a series of films in which, repeatedly, a small group of people in severely circumscribed circumstances worked their way through a dramatic situation. *Men Without Women* (1930), his first film for Ford, reveals the pattern in its naked simplicity: fourteen men trapped in a submarine awaiting rescue.

In the light of Nichols's theorizing and customary practice, it is interesting to see what he made of O'Flaherty's *Informer*. The central dramatic conflict of the novel he understood to be 'a man against a group of people'.[77] Already we can see the necessary simplifications at work. For cinematic purposes this struggle had to be given a larger scope than the betrayal of a radical communist or labour group. Hence the decision to make it the 'Irish Revolution Easter trouble [*sic*]'[78] – a phrase that is a marvel of historical imprecision but which conflates all the signs of Irish rebelliousness for an American audience. Gypo as hunted man was an ideal subject to demonstrate the theory of reaction rather than action.

This much decided, Nichols got to work with his customary skill to produce a film script that was long regarded as a model of its kind. George Bluestone, in his groundbreaking study of adaptation, devoted a chapter to a detailed analysis of the materials carried over or deleted from O'Flaherty's book and declared the cumulative changes so great that the result was a new species.[79] This is surely going too far; despite its many alterations, the Ford–Nichols rendition is in the main faithful to the novel in a way that is not true of the Robison version. The most startling transformation is in the character of Dan Gallagher (played by Preston Foster). In the novel he is a complex, if repellent, killer whose ideology and motives for action are unclear even to himself. In the film he is an eminently rational, fair-minded, trench-coated revolutionary leader who has earned the respect of everybody and who deploys a masterful pipe to prove it (Nichols's script introduces him with the phrase 'a fine type'). There can be little doubt, however, that this clean-cut hero ultimately derives from Ford's extravagant idealization of the IRA. (He would later even try to cajole Sean O'Casey into changing the ending of a proposed film version of *The Plough and the Stars* to fit his providential view of Irish history.)

More than anything else, it was the expressionist styling of the film (what Nichols described as the 'stylized symbolism [that] was the key to the whole thing'[80]) that brought critical attention and popular acclaim. This, too, was largely Nichols's doing, though doubtless the matter had been decided in a general way in the course of preliminary discussions with the director. Nichols, however, believed that it was he rather than Ford who pushed the idea of stylization hardest, while readily conceding Ford's mastery of the technique:

> I never heard Ford mention *The Last Laugh* or *Dr Caligari's Cabinet*, but it is very likely he had absorbed what they had to give in the way of new film ideas. He wanted some distortion in the sets from the beginning, and I don't think Van Polglase (or the rigid ideas of a major studio itself) gave him as much of this as he desired.[81]

Nichols has left a disarming description of the clever way symbols were chosen and then concealed in the narrative like currants in a bun. So deliberate and mechanical was the procedure as he describes it that it is possible to draw up a table of equivalencies along the following lines:

> The fog = moral confusion
> The blind man = dark conscience
> The tapping stick = the pursuit of conscience
> The poster = betrayal
> The ship = freedom
> The three coins = guilt
> Clocks and the blowing wind = fate
> The hat = security
> Etc., etc.

It is just with regard to the employment of symbolism that we can mark the difference between the rather rigid and calculating approach of Nichols and the fluid mastery of Ford's direction. Three examples will bring out the contrast.

One of the most magical moments in all cinema is the scene in *The Informer* where Margot Grahame as Katie Madden is transformed in an instant from a statuesque Madonna into a Magdalene. Ford accomplishes this with extraordinary economy. Katie simply throws back her heavy enveloping shawl to reveal a fetching hat perched on the back of her head. There is no hint of this in the script, which is leaden and overelaborate on this point.

Nichols himself drew attention in his letter to Lindsay Anderson to two further episodes where Ford, together with his cameraman Joe August, seized the moment on set to go far beyond what he had scripted. When Gypo is first called before Dan Gallagher to account for his movements, Gallagher crumples the 'wanted' poster in his hands and throws it in the fire. Gypo is forced to watch as it slowly blackens and is drawn up the chimney by the draft. It is a powerful moment, not readily decipherable in terms of a ready-made toolkit of symbols (Nichols had Gallagher burn the offending poster before Gypo enters the room). More thoroughgoing still was Ford's management of the interrogation scene, where Gypo accuses the innocent tailor of informing on Frankie McPhillip. Nichols had written a very elaborate scenario crammed with symbolism and superimposed photography in an effort to portray Gypo's schizoid state of mind. Ford threw it out completely and adopted a brilliant, if dictatorial, approach to directing Victor McLaglen. Legend has it that he got McLaglen drunk on set and shot the scene while the actor was scarcely able to talk or walk. The legend credits Ford with a lack of subtlety. In fact he encouraged McLaglen to party the night before, on the grounds that there would be nothing for him to do for a couple of days. The following morning he called him in very early and forced him to rehearse the trial scene, which Joe August surreptitiously filmed. McLaglen's hesitations, stumbling delivery and ad-libbing are far more effective in rendering the confused state of the informer than Nichols's elaborately designed *mise-en-scène*.

These three instances demonstrate Ford's way with a Nichols script. He tightened it up on set, cut dialogue and seized whatever momentary inspiration the process offered. *The Informer* was shot in a mere twenty-seven days, from 11 February to 15 March, and was the easiest film the director ever made. The rapidity with which Ford moved from scene to scene and the sureness of touch which he demonstrated were in large part due to the obsessively detailed script supplied by Nichols.

A film, of course, is vastly more than a dialectic between a director and a writer. All through his career John Ford gathered around him a virtual stock company of actors and technical staff whom he could both bully and blarney into delivering first-rate performances. The key personnel on the set of *The Informer* were lead actor Victor McLaglen, cinematographer Joseph H. August and composer/arranger Max Steiner.

McLaglen (1886–1959) appealed to Ford not only as an actor but as a soldier with the kind of extravagant picaresque life that the director could only envy and occasionally fantasize about for himself.

The son of an Anglican bishop, McLaglen had been a boy ensign with a cavalry regiment in the Boer War, a captain during World War I, and ended his military career as Provost Marshal of Baghdad under Allenby. Between times he had taken to prize-fighting in Canada (he weighed in at 225 lb and 6'3" against world heavyweight champion Jack Johnson) and performing in circuses and vaudeville. He had no formal training as an actor and, insofar as he can be described as having an acting style at all, that style is early expressionist with a penchant for very large crude gestures and furious grimaces. The actor in the expressionist tradition is a puppet in the hands of the all-powerful director. This suited McLaglen's narrow range and he could get by in silent films. His limitations, however, were to become painfully obvious as the Stanislavsky method took hold in Hollywood and elsewhere. He was an actor whose body and voice, as Rodney Farnsworth remarks, 'function[ed] best at their extreme'.[82] Ford had no illusions about him as a performer and cruelly goaded him on set to produce those extravagant responses for which McLaglen is best remembered – as the berserk sergeant in *The Lost Patrol* (1934) and Gypo Nolan in *The Informer*. The bizarre, not to say paranoid, world of both films were perfectly suited to his histrionic talents. Because *The Informer* was an ensemble piece there were other factors besides Ford's direction at work on his performance. The shambling gait of the Gypo character, for example, was largely dictated by Max Steiner's musical score. Remarkably, the 'Gypo leitmotif' with its heavily accented rhythms was composed before the shooting schedule began and Ford rehearsed and shot McLaglen in synchronization with it. Farnsworth's tribute to the director's ability to choose exactly the right actors for these ensemble works is just: 'McLaglen's absence from the director's vision would be like a Franz Hals low-life canvas without its drunken, wide-mouthed clown.'[83]

And not only actors. One of the great careers of the 'Golden Age' of Hollywood was that of the cinematographer Joseph H. August. Ford first teamed up with him in 1925 for *The Fighting Heart*, a boxing film also starring McLaglen, who had come to California the previous year. August's progress through Hollywood from 1913 onwards raises the intriguing question of the extent to which expressionist lighting was a native growth, quite independent of developments in Germany. From early on he experimented with chiaroscuro and dramatic contrasts of a kind that, too easily perhaps, we ascribe solely to the German masters. What was not in doubt was his willingness to experiment and the freedom he earned to do so by his prolific output. One of his more memorable accomplishments with Ford was on the set of *Men Without Women*, where he filmed the submersion of the submarine by mounting a camera in a booth on the conning-tower. His work on *The Informer* was equally daring. He sought to make most of the lighting diegetic (lighting as part of the film's story world). A principle effect aimed at in the film was the production of 'halations', meaning the diffusion of local fog around high lights. Dudley Nichols recalled that August 'never hesitated to shoot directly at a sun-arc, if Ford wanted to try it – and Ford had an experimental mind. Most studio cameramen refused to take chances, fearing censure from their department heads.'[84] Were one to bracket the German expressionist influences on the film and look at it anew solely through Joe August's camerawork, *The Informer*, shot entirely as a night piece, emerges as a startling precursor of 1940s *film noir*.

Even more prodigious than August in his output was composer and arranger Max Steiner. Between 1929 and 1936 he was music director for RKO Radio Pictures and during that period alone he was responsible for the music of one hundred and thirty-seven films. While working on *The Informer* he managed to squeeze in a further six RKO productions! His work has been extensively studied for its contribution to Hollywood classical cinema, but what is overlooked is the way his score for *The Informer* returns that film to melodrama, even in the strictly etymological sense of the word as a 'drama-with-songs'. At the diegetic level alone, 'The Rose of Tralee' is sung by a street singer, 'The Minstrel Boy' at Frankie's wake and, quite wonderfully, 'Believe Me If All Those Endearing Young Charms' in the brothel scene. Yet another ballad which weaves its way through the film is 'The Wearing of the Green', sung in unison by Frankie and Gypo to obvious purpose, and the melody of 'Yankee Doodle Dandy' plays over Katie's street scene to symbolize the longed-for escape to America. In this heavily saturated Irish musical environment, the fragment of 'Rule Britannia' in a minor key which accompanies Gypo's encounter with the 'wanted' poster helps to resolve the ambiguity or plain blank incompetence of McLaglen's performance at that point.

A certain effort of the historical imagination is necessary to capture a sense of the originality and excitement of Steiner's score. Apart from his employment of Wagnerian motifs for major characters and his blending of folk tunes and original music, his hallmark characteristic as a film composer was 'Mickey Mousing' – so-called after the practice of writing musical cues for onscreen action in Disney cartoons. Today this is widely disparaged as redundancy, but just how effective it was – and difficult to manage – is shown by Steiner's own comments:

> There was a sequence towards the end of the picture in which McLaglen is in a cell and water is dripping on him. This is just before he escapes and is killed. I had a certain musical effect I wanted to use for this. I wanted to catch each of these drops musically. The property man and I worked for days trying to regulate the water tank so it dripped in tempo and so I could accompany it. This took a great deal of time and thought because a dripping faucet doesn't always drip in the same rhythm. We finally mastered it, and I believe it was one of the things that won me the award. People were fascinated trying to figure out how we managed to catch every drop.[85]

As noted above, some of the music for *The Informer* was written in advance of the actual filming, and this allowed Ford to pace

McLaglen's movements to the score. This was exactly the kind of collaborative effort that Dudley Nichols and Ford prized – and that they were never to achieve again.

Hollywood Cemetery

One of the least acknowledged, if powerful, motives for writing a book is to have the last word on a particular subject *in print*. This was certainly among O'Flaherty's reasons for writing his West of Ireland novel *Skerrett*, where he delivered the *coup de grâce* to clerical, legal and popular oral accounts of the troubled career of Master O'Callaghan on the Aran Islands. We may suspect that a similar motive prompted the writing of *Hollywood Cemetery*, his brilliant exposé of the celluloid city of the 1940s. It is one of the most assured of all O'Flaherty's novels and demonstrates unexpected gifts for burlesque and sustained satire. Ford appears as the director Bud Tracy and Nichols as Sam Gunn, Big Chief of Scenarists. O'Flaherty is the hopelessly compromised Irish writer Brian Carey. Part of the strength of the book lies in the way in which O'Flaherty sends up himself as much as anybody else. The cemetery of the title derives from a supposed article on Hollywood in the communist newspaper *Proletarian Power* (the novel is astonishingly post-modern in places in the way in which it clashes a variety of discourses to show the constructed nature of reality): 'Hollywood is a cemetery where the remains of present-day bourgeois intellectuals are buried, after being fattened, like the sacrificial victims in ancient Mexico on enormous salaries, only to have their hearts plucked out and eaten by the Moguls of modern mammon.' O'Flaherty is clearly working out of the tradition of inherited dissent that afflicts the sub-genre known as the Hollywood Novel (Fitzgerald, West, Waugh, Didion), for any final account of the Ford–Nichols collaboration on his own *Informer* has to acknowledge the vitality and indeed the artistic accomplishments of the Hollywood version. As O'Flaherty commented elsewhere, in the epigraph that frames this present study:

'Oh well, so much has been done to *The Informer* that another little sting can't matter.' Such a powerfully mythogenic text has proved itself to be a far more resilient – and inspirational – work of art than its author could ever have imagined.

APPENDIX

NARRATIVE SYNOPSIS OF ROBISON'S *INFORMER* (1929)

The original script breaks up the action into four parts and provides a convenient scheme to manage the complex scenario.

Part the First
In a smoke-filled room at Headquarters, Gallagher announces to the Party members that their activities will be peaceful from now on. Promptly, from a window across the street, the Other Side opens up on the meeting with a machine pistol and attempts to break in by the downstairs door. Katie Fox, the only woman present, loads the guns while the battle rages. In the mêlée, Francis McPhillip shoots dead the Chief of Police. Gallagher, seconded by Katie, orders McPhillip to take to the hills to preserve the Party.

Part the Second
Out in his cavern in the mountains, McPhillip, very much the worse for wear, receives a message from the Party and his fare to America. He must not return to the city, where there are posters up offering a reward for his capture. But he cannot resist visiting Katie in Church Street before making his final farewells to his mother.

McPhillip wants Katie to come with him to America but she tells him that things are not as they were. She is now in love with Gypo Nolan. Footsteps on the stairs announce the arrival of Gypo with a bunch of violets 'for me own Katie'. Katie hides the importunate McPhillip, who is later observed escaping from the house by Gypo. He accuses Katie of deception and in a fit of pique she responds by telling Gypo that she loves McPhillip and will indeed go with him to America.

McPhillip makes his farewells to his white-haired mother when Katie arrives to tell him that he has been seen by Gypo and hence should keep out of his rival's way. Unknown to both, they are observed by Gypo who jumps to the conclusion that they are indeed going off together. He betrays McPhillip to the police. In a finely managed ironic transition a policeman takes down Gypo's details in long hand; cut to McPhillip writing an explanatory, friendly letter to Gypo.

McPhillip is shot by the police while attempting to escape across the rooftops. Gallagher initiates an enquiry on behalf of the Party. There is an informer among them. Gypo has been seen by a whore at the police station and so suspicion immediately falls on him.

When Gypo and Katie meet up in the street she explains that she never intended to go to America: Gypo made her angry and she was just hitting back at him. And she wasn't hiding McPhillip from him but from the police. Gypo admits to her that he is the informer. But Katie loves him and will stand by her man. Gypo must act normally, so she leads him to a dancehall.

Part the Third

Gypo and Katie are accosted by Gallagher and his two henchmen, Murphy and Mulholland, in the dancehall. Gypo is asked to agree that 'the rat who informed on McPhillip deserves to die'. He is detailed to convey the Party's sympathies directly to the dead man's mother. Gallagher puts a tail (Mulholland) on him. Katie is ordered to attend a meeting of the Party that night.

'You were my son's best friend,' says Mother McPhillip to Gypo at the wake house. Gypo pulls out his handkerchief and with it a wad of notes. Everybody, including Mulholland, recognizes that this is the blood money.

At the Party meeting Katie is interrogated by Captain Gallagher. It is just at this point that the film breaks into sound. She lies in defence of her lover until Mulholland arrives to announce that the informer has given himself away, whereupon Katie denounces Gypo. She tells Gallagher that he is at her place, not heading for the hills as everybody supposes. The benign interpretation of this is that she is trying to buy time for her lover.

Gallagher accompanies Katie into her rooms in search of the fugitive. Katie offers herself to him in exchange for Gypo's life, but he is unyielding as he realizes that she has conned him. Meanwhile, Gypo is at Green Street Railway Station waiting for the ticket office to open. Also at the station is the barmaid Bessie, whom we have seen earlier drinking with Gypo. She is fleeing from her cynical cigar-chomping employer, who arrives just in time to claim the money she owes him for board and lodging. (Their relationship is clearly that of prostitute and pimp.) Touched by her plight, Gypo pays her debt with all the money he has left; she signs a photograph of herself as a memento of his goodness.

The members of the Party are waiting for Gypo outside the station. He is taken and thrown unconscious into a lorry. Murphy relieves him of his pocket book, which includes the signed picture of Bessie. The others kick him in the ribs. With the proverbial supreme effort, Gypo revives and throws himself from the moving lorry. The action sequence which follows is very confusing, but what seems to be intended is that Gypo escapes into a railway tunnel. His pursuers hold back when they hear an oncoming train. The train comes to a halt at the tunnel entrance and the stoker announces: 'We ran over a man back there!'

Part the Fourth – Finale

Katie is asleep in her bedroom when, Nosferatu-like, a figure climbs in her window. It is Gypo. 'Sleep, Gypo – you are safe here,' she says, as she goes off to seek police protection for him. But waiting for her on the landing is Captain Gallagher with news that Gypo has been run over by a train. She is well rid of him and he demonstrates the point by handing her Bessie's signed photograph: 'Men don't give every penny they have got to a girl for nothing, and that is what he did.' Furious, Katie betrays Gypo by throwing open the bedroom door where he lies asleep. Gallagher asks her to keep him there until he gets the boys round.

Gypo awakens and reveals the casual way he gave the girl at the station his money as an act of reparation. Katie realizes that she has needlessly betrayed her lover. Just then there is a knock at the door. They assume it is the assassins and prepare for the worst. It is the postman with the letter addressed to Gypo from McPhillip in which he states he has said goodbye to Katie forever. Gypo's betrayal, too, was needless.

The comrades duly arrive. Katie pleads with Gypo to save himself, but he goes out to meet his fate, locking her inside. Gallagher shoots him as he descends the staircase. He crawls to the church opposite, where he begs forgiveness from McPhillip's mother. In hysterical gaiety he calls out 'Francie, Francie, your mother has forgiven me,' and dies with the shadow of the crucifix across his prone body. [*Ends*]

CREDITS

Title:	**The Informer**
Director:	John Ford
Release Year:	1935
Production Company:	RKO Radio Pictures
Country:	USA

Cast:

Victor McLaglen	Gypo Nolan
Heather Angel	Mary McPhillip
Preston Foster	Dan Gallagher
Margot Grahame	Katie Madden
Wallace Ford	Frankie McPhillip
Una O'Connor	Mrs McPhillip
J. M. Kerrigan	Terry
Joseph Sawyer	Bartley Mulholland
Neil Fitzgerald	Tommy Connor
Donald Meek	Pat Mulligan
D'Arcy Corrigan	The Blind Man
Leo McCable	Dennis Donahue
Gaylord Pendleton	Daley
Francis Ford	'Judge' Flynn
May Boley	Madame Betty
Grizelda Harvey	British officer
Jack Mulhall	Look-out at wake
Robert Parrish	Young soldier

Credits:

John Ford	Director
Cliff Reid	Associate Producer
Edward O'Fearna	Assistant Director
Dudley Nichols	Screenplay
Liam O'Flaherty	Script Contribution
Liam O'Flaherty	Based on the novel by
Joseph August	Photography
George Hively	Editor
Van Nest Polglase	Art Director
Charles M. Kirk	Art Director (Associate)
Julia Heron	Set Decorator
Walter Plunkett	Costumes

Max Steiner	Music
Hugh McDowell Jr.	Recorder
Philip Faulkner	Recorder
Elizabeth McGaffey	Research
S. Barrett McCormack	Press Agent

| Running Time: | 91 mins |
| Colour Code: | Black/White |

Title: **The Informer**
Director: Arthur Robison
Release Year: 1929
Production Company: British International Pictures
Country: Great Britain

Cast:

Lars Hanson	Gypo Nolan
Carl Harbord	Francis McPhillip
Lya De Putti	Katie Fox
Daisy Campbell	Mrs McPhillip
Warwick Ward	Dan Gallagher
Ellen Pollock	Prostitute
Janice Adair	Bessie
Dennis Wyndham	Murphy
Craighall Sherry	Mulholland
Johnny Butt	Publican
Mickey Brantford	
Ray Milland	

Credits:

Arthur Robison	Director
John Harlow	Associate Director
Benn Levy	Dialogue
Rolf E. Vanloo and Arthur Robison	Screenplay
Liam O'Flaherty	Original novel
Werner Brandes	Photography
Theodor Sparkull	Photography
Emile De Ruelle	Production Editor
J. Elder Wills	Art Director

Running Time:	83 mins
Field Length:	7392 ft or 2254 mtrs
Colour Code:	Black/White

Notes

1   Liam O'Flaherty to Kitty Tailer, 25 July 1961, in *The Letters of Liam O'Flaherty*, ed. A. A. Kelly (Dublin: Wolfhound Press, 1996), p. 362.

2   Liam O'Flaherty to Edward Garnett, 18 September 1924, in Kelly, pp. 101–102; and Liam O'Flaherty, *Shame the Devil* (1934; Dublin: Wolfhound Press, 1981), pp. 190–191.

3   Francis MacManus, 'Imaginative Literature and the Revolution', in *The Irish Struggle 1916–1926*, ed. Desmond Williams (London: Routledge & Kegan Paul, 1966), p. 25.

4   Liam O'Flaherty to Kitty Tailer, 10 July 1969, in Kelly, p. 411.

5   See René Girard, *Violence and the Sacred*, trans. Patrick Gregory (Baltimore: Johns Hopkins University Press, 1979).

6   Liam O'Flaherty, *The Informer* (1925; London/Dublin: Jonathan Cape/Wolfhound Press, 1999), p. 7.

7   Mike Milotte, *Communism in Modern Ireland: the Pursuit of the Workers' Republic Since 1916* (Dublin: Gill & Macmillan, 1984), p. 57.

8   O'Flaherty, *The Informer*, p. 233.

9   O'Flaherty, *The Informer*, p. 233.

10   Anonymous, *Hollywood Reporter*, Vol. 328, No. 19 (1993), pp. 4, 58.

11   Liam O'Flaherty to Edward Garnett, April 1924, in Kelly, p. 86.

12   *Editors' note*: According to Brendan Bradshaw, Irish revisionism originally developed in two phases: firstly, in the aftermath of independence, as an essentially 'value-free' discourse which was sceptical of nationalist ideology; and secondly, after the 1960s, as a kind of studied iconoclasm which privileged irony as a rhetorical weapon for debunking perceived nationalist mythologies. Presumably it is the latter phase which Professor Sheeran is referring to here. See Brendan Bradshaw, 'Nationalism and Historical Scholarship in Modern Ireland', in *Interpreting Irish History: the Debate on Historical Revisionism*, ed. Ciaran Brady (Dublin: Irish Academic Press, 1994), pp. 191–216.

13   J. Bowyer Bell, *The Secret Army: a History of the IRA, 1915–1970*, 3rd edition (Dublin: Poolbeg, 1998), p. 25.

14   Kevin O'Higgins, 'Three Years' Hard Labour', quoted in Michael Hopkinson, *Green Against Green: the Irish Civil War* (Dublin: Gill & Macmillan, 1988), p. 52.

15   O'Flaherty, *Shame the Devil*, pp. 35–36.

16   Milotte, p. 59.

17   Liam O'Flaherty, 'Autobiographical Note', in *Ten Contemporaries*, ed. John Gawsworth (London: Joiner & Steele, 1934), p. 42; reproduced as 'Apprenticeship as a Writer', in *Liam O'Flaherty: a Study of the Short Fiction*, by James M. Cahalan (Boston, Mass.: Twayne, 1991), p. 93.

18   Liam O'Flaherty to Edward Garnett, 17 January 1927, in Kelly, p. 173.

19   Liam O'Flaherty to the editor of the *Irish Statesman*, 18 October 1924, in Kelly, pp. 105–106.

20   John Ford to Mary Ford, undated, quoted in Scott Eyman, *Print the Legend: the Life and Times of John Ford* (New York: Simon & Schuster, 1999), p. 70.

21   John Ford to Mary Ford, undated, quoted in Dan Ford, *The Unquiet Man: the Life of John Ford* (London: William Kimber, 1982), p. 23.

22   Frank Pakenham, *Peace by Ordeal: an Account, from First-hand Sources, of the Negotiation and Signature of the Anglo-Irish Treaty* (Cork: Mercier Press, 1960), p. 255.

23   Dan Ford, p. 23.

24   *Editors' note*: For a slightly different interpretation of Ford's account of the burning of Spiddal, see Luke Gibbons, *The Quiet Man*, Ireland into Film series (Cork: Cork UP/Film Institute of Ireland, 2002), pp. 42–44.

Prof Gearóid Ó Tuathaigh adds: 'On 14 May 1921 a local IRA unit, probably no more than 9–10 men, ambushed Crown forces in Spiddal. The precise details of the composition or designation of the Crown forces is not clear, although two of them were certainly wounded. The ambush caused surprise, as the area had not been "active" in the guerrilla campaign previously. A few days later Crown forces carried out reprisals in the Spiddal area and indeed further afield, over the hill as far as Moycullen. A number of houses were burned in the neighbourhood of Spiddal, specifically those of known or suspected IRA activists/sympathisers. Among the houses burned was the Thornton's. Another house burned belonged to the Costello family. There is no specific mention of a Feeney house being burned (though this does not preclude Feeneys being among those who suffered). The total number of houses burned is not clear. It is reasonable to assume that IRA activists – including those actually involved in the ambush – would have gone into hiding, perhaps in the (largely inaccessible) hill and bog areas outside of Spiddal.

Clearly, Ford exaggerated and embellished his account, and rendered highly melodramatic the incident in Spiddal and its aftermath. But the ambush and reprisal did actually take place (though in May 1921), and cannot be dismissed as mere invention. References to the Black and Tans and surveillance may be embellishments, and the picture of Spiddal village having been burned to the ground may have been grossly exaggerated. However, the locals are likely to have spoken of the reprisals in very outraged terms – precisely because there had been few, if any, such incidents in the locality – and this entire episode must have been vividly discussed during Ford's visit.' (Source: Information provided by Cormac Ó Comhraí, completing an M.A. thesis in History at NUI, Galway (2002), on the intelligence aspects of the Irish War of Independence.)

The editors are indebted to Prof Ó Tuathaigh and Mr Ó Comhraí for this information.

25   See Albert Memmi, *The Colonizer and the Colonized*, trans. Howard Greenfield (London: Earthscan, 1980), p. 202.
26   Jean Mitry, 'Interview with [John] Ford', *Cahiers du Cinema*, Vol. 45 (March 1955), p. 9.
27   Alan Spiegel, *Visual Consciousness in Film and the Modern Novel* (Charlottesville: University Press of Virginia, 1976), pp. 76–77. The Joyce passage comes from Stanislaus Joyce, *My Brother's Keeper*, ed. Richard Ellmann (New York: Viking, 1964), p. 90.
28   Denis Donoghue, 'Preface', *The Informer* (New York: Harcourt Brace, 1980), p. xii.
29   Charles Eidsvik, 'Demonstrating Film Influence', *Literature/Film Quarterly*, Vol. 1, No. 2 (1973), p. 117.
30   O'Flaherty, *Shame the Devil*, p. 58.
31   O'Flaherty, *Shame the Devil*, p. 59.
32   'I expect to go ahead with my novel now. I am going to try and sell it serially and for film. I think it would work well on the films at least': Liam O'Flaherty to Edward Garnett, April 1924, in Kelly, p. 86.
33   Liam O'Flaherty to Edward Garnett, 7 July 1924, in Kelly, p. 95.
34   Liam O'Flaherty to Edward Garnett, 20 January 1925, in Kelly, p. 112.
35   Liam O'Flaherty to Edward Garnett, 20 January 1925, in Kelly, pp. 112–113.
36   O'Flaherty, *Shame the Devil*, pp. 190–191.
37   W. M. Paul, 'The Crisis in Germany', *Workers' Republic* (2 September 1922), p. 3.
38   O'Flaherty, *Shame the Devil*, pp. 189–190.

39   O'Flaherty, *The Informer*, pp. 181–182.

40   O'Flaherty, *The Informer*, pp. 69–70.

41   O'Flaherty, *The Informer*, pp. 143, 157.

42   See Klaus Theweleit, *Male Fantasies* (Minneapolis: University of Minnesota Press, 1990), for a discussion of the significance of such objects in Weimar Germany.

43   There is an excellent chapter on melodrama in *The Cinema Book*, ed. Pam Cook (London: BFI, 1985), pp. 73–84.

44   These terms are employed in James L. Smith, *Melodrama* (London: Methuen, 1977).

45   Daniel Gerould, 'Russian Formalist Theories of Melodrama', *Journal of American Culture* (Spring 1978), p. 154.

46   Liam O'Flaherty to Edward Garnett, 18 September 1924, in Kelly, pp. 101–102.

47   O'Flaherty, *The Informer*, p. 122.

48   Rick Altman, *The American Film Musical* (Bloomington: Indiana University Press, 1987), p. 21.

49   O'Flaherty, *The Informer*, pp. 266–267.

50   Donoghue, p. x.

51   See Thomas Elsaesser, 'Tales of Sound and Fury: Observations on the Family Melodrama', in *Home Is Where the Heart Is: Studies in Melodrama and the Woman's Film*, ed. Christine Gledhill (London: BFI, 1987), p. 68.

52   The point is made with regard to German cinema by Thomas Elsaesser in 'Social Mobility and the Fantastic: German Silent Cinema', *Wide Angle*, Vol. 5, No. 2 (1982), p. 20.

53   Elsaesser, 'Social Mobility and the Fantastic', p. 19.

54   Dan Ford, p. 42.

55   E. E. Barrett, 'Meet De Putti Lady', *The Picturegoer*, Vol. 17, No. 100 (1929), p. 25.

56   Rolf E. Vanloo and Artur (*sic*) Robison, '*The Informer* (*Die Nacht nach dem Verrat*), freely adapted from the novel by Liam O'Flaherty', Screenplay (1928?), Irish Film Institute Ms., p. 69.

57   Anonymous [Review], *Close Up*, Vol. 6, No. 2 (1930), pp. 159, 160.

58   Vanloo and Robison, p. 54.

59   Paul Rotha, *The Film Till Now: a Survey of the Cinema* (New York: Cape & Harrison Smith, 1930), p. 201.

60   Rotha, p. 229.

61   Liam O'Leary, 'Arthur Robison', in *International Dictionary of Films*

and Filmmakers, Vol. 2: Directors/Filmmakers, ed. Christopher Lyon (London: Papermac, 1987), pp. 455–456.

62 See Thomas Elsaesser, *Weimar Cinema and After: Germany's Historical Imaginary* (London: Routledge, 2000), for a powerful exploration of these themes.

63 Vanloo and Robison, p. 73.

64 Mary Manning [Review], '*The Informer*', *Irish Statesman* (30 November 1929), p. 256.

65 The judgement of the official film censor is quoted in Louisa Burns-Bisogno, *Censoring Irish Nationalism: the British, Irish and American Suppression of Republican Images in Film and Television, 1909–95* (Jefferson, NC, and London: McFarland, 1997), p. 77. There seems to be some confusion here between the censor's dismissal of the Robison version and the later attempt to censor the Ford version.

66 John Pym, ed. '*The Informer*', in *Time Out*, 9th edition (Harmondsworth: Penguin, 2001), p. 524.

67 Andrew Sarris, '*You Ain't Heard Nothin' Yet': the American Talking Film – History and Memory 1927–1949* (New York: Oxford University Press, 1998), p. 181.

68 Za Nichols, '*The Informer* Radioscript', Gen. Mss. Misc. Group 968, F–1, Beinecke Rare Book and Manuscript Library, Yale University, pp. 1–2.

69 Tag Gallagher, *John Ford: the Man and his Films* (Berkeley: University of California, 1986), p. 122.

70 Dan Ford, p. 84.

71 Dudley Nichols to Lindsay Anderson, April 22 1953, in Lindsay Anderson, *About John Ford . . .* (London: Plexus, 1981), p. 238.

72 Dudley Nichols, 'The Making of a Scenario', *National Board of Review Magazine* (March 1939), p. 4.

73 Dudley Nichols, 'The Writer and the Film', *Theatre Arts* (October 1943), p. 599.

74 Dudley Nichols to the Gentlemen of the Academy (February? 1936), quoted in Nancy Lynn Schwartz, *The Hollywood Writers' Wars* (New York: Knopf, 1982), pp. 51–52.

75 Dudley Nichols, 'Film Writing', *Theatre Arts* (December 1942), p. 773.

76 Nichols, 'The Writer and the Film', p. 594.

77 Nichols, 'The Making of a Scenario', p. 4.

78 Nichols, 'The Making of a Scenario', p. 5.

79 George Bluestone, *Novels into Film* (Baltimore: Johns Hopkins University Press, 1957), pp. 65–90.

80 Nichols to Lindsay Anderson, p. 239.

81 Nichols to Lindsay Anderson, p. 239.

82 Rodney Farnsworth, 'Victor McLaglen', in *International Dictionary of Films and Filmmakers, Vol. 3: Actors and Actresses*, ed. Amy L. Unterburger (New York: St James, 1997), p. 800.

83 Farnsworth, p. 800.

84 Nichols to Lindsay Anderson, pp. 239–240.

85 Max Steiner, quoted in Kathryn Kalinak, *Settling the Score: Music and the Classical Hollywood Film* (Madison and London: University of Wisconsin, 1992), p. 129.

Bibliography

Altman, Rick. *The American Film Musical*. Bloomington: Indiana University Press, 1987.

Anderson, Lindsay. *About John Ford . . .* London: Plexus, 1981.

Anonymous. *Hollywood Reporter*, Vol. 328, No. 19 (1993): 4, 58.

Anonymous [Review]. '*The Informer* (*Die Nacht nach dem Verrat*)'. *Close Up*, Vol. 6, No. 2 (1930): 159–160.

Barrett, E. E. 'Meet De Putti Lady'. *The Picturegoer*, Vol. 17, No. 100 (1929): 25.

Bell, J. Bowyer. *The Secret Army: a History of the IRA, 1915–1970*. 3rd edition. Dublin: Poolbeg, 1998.

Bluestone, George. *Novels into Film*. Baltimore: Johns Hopkins University Press, 1957.

Bradshaw, Brendan. 'Nationalism and Historical Scholarship in Modern Ireland', *Interpreting Irish History: the Debate on Historical Revisionism*, ed. Ciaran Brady. Dublin: Irish Academic Press, 1994. 191–216.

Brook, Peter. *The Melodramatic Imagination: Balzac, Henry James, Melodrama, and the Mode of Excess*. New Haven: Yale University Press, 1976.

Burns-Bisogno, Louisa. *Censoring Irish Nationalism: the British, Irish and American Suppression of Republican Images in Film and Television, 1909–95*. Jefferson, NC, and London: McFarland, 1997.

Cook, Pam. Ed. *The Cinema Book*. London: BFI, 1985.

Donoghue, Denis. 'Preface'. *The Informer*. New York: Harcourt Brace, 1980.

Eidsvik, Charles. 'Demonstrating Film Influence'. *Literature/Film Quarterly*, Vol. 1, No. 2 (1973).

Elsaesser, Thomas. 'Social Mobility and the Fantastic: German Silent Cinema'. *Wide Angle*, Vol. 5, No. 2 (1982).

——. 'Tales of Sound and Fury: Observations on the Family Melodrama', *Home Is Where the Heart Is: Studies in Melodrama and the Woman's Film*, Ed. Christine Gledhill. London: BFI, 1987.

——. *Weimar Cinema and After: Germany's Historical Imaginary*. London: Routledge, 2000.

Eyman, Scott. *Print the Legend: the Life and Times of John Ford*. New York: Simon & Schuster, 1999.

Farnsworth, Rodney. 'Victor McLaglen'. *International Dictionary of Films and Filmmakers, Vol. 3: Actors and Actresses*. Amy L. Unterburger. New York: St James, 1997. 800.

Ford, Dan. *The Unquiet Man: the Life of John Ford*. London: William Kimber, 1982.

89

Gallagher, Tag. *John Ford: the Man and his Films*. Berkeley: University of California, 1986.

Gerould, Daniel. 'Russian Formalist Theories of Melodrama'. *Journal of American Culture* (Spring 1978).

Girard, René. *Violence and the Sacred*. Trans. Patrick Gregory. Baltimore: Johns Hopkins University Press, 1979.

Hopkinson, Michael. *Green Against Green: the Irish Civil War*. Dublin: Gill & Macmillan, 1988.

Joyce, Stanislaus. *My Brother's Keeper*. Ed. Richard Ellmann. New York: Viking, 1964.

Kalinak, Kathryn. *Settling the Score: Music and the Classical Hollywood Film*. Madison and London: University of Wisconsin, 1992.

MacManus, Francis. 'Imaginative Literature and the Revolution'. *The Irish Struggle 1916–1926*. Desmond Williams. London: Routledge & Kegan Paul, 1966. 19–30.

Manning, Mary [Review]. '*The Informer*'. *Irish Statesman* (30 November 1929): 256.

Memmi, Albert. *The Colonizer and the Colonized*. Trans. Howard Greenfield. London: Earthscan, 1980.

Milotte, Mike. *Communism in Modern Ireland: the Pursuit of the Workers' Republic Since 1916*. Dublin: Gill & Macmillan, 1984.

Mitry, Jean. 'Interview with [John] Ford'. *Cahiers du Cinema*, Vol. 45 (March 1955).

Nichols, Dudley. 'The Making of a Scenario'. *National Board of Review Magazine* (March 1939).

——. 'Film Writing'. *Theatre Arts* (December 1942).

——. 'The Writer and the Film'. *Theatre Arts* (October 1943).

Nichols, Za. '*The Informer* Radioscript'. Gen. Mss. Misc. Group 968, F–1. Beinecke Rare Book and Manuscript Library, Yale University.

Ó Comhraí, Cormac. Unpublished MA thesis on the intelligence aspects of the Irish War of Independence. NUI, Galway (2002).

O'Flaherty, Liam. *The Informer*. 1925; London/Dublin: Jonathan Cape/Wolfhound Press, 1999.

——. *Shame the Devil*. 1934; Dublin: Wolfhound Press, 1981.

——. 'Autobiographical Note'. *Ten Contemporaries*, ed. John Gawsworth. London: Joiner & Steele, 1934. 139–143. Reproduced as 'Apprenticeship as a Writer'. *Liam O'Flaherty: a Study of the Short Fiction*. James M. Cahalan Boston: Twayne, 1991. 92–95.

——. *Hollywood Cemetery: a Novel*. London: Gollancz, 1935.

——. *The Letters of Liam O'Flaherty*. Ed. A. A. Kelly. Dublin: Wolfhound Press, 1996.

O'Leary, Liam. 'Arthur Robison', in *International Dictionary of Films and Filmmakers, Vol. 2: Directors/Filmmakers*, ed. Christopher Lyon. London: Papermac, 1987. 455–456.

Pakenham, Frank. *Peace by Ordeal: an Account, from First-hand Sources, of the Negotiation and Signature of the Anglo-Irish Treaty*. Cork: Mercier Press, 1960.

Paul, W. M. 'The Crisis in Germany'. *Workers' Republic* (2 September 1922): 3.

Pym, John. Ed. *'The Informer'. Time Out.* 9th edition. Harmondsworth: Penguin, 2001. 524.

Rotha, Paul. *The Film Till Now: a Survey of the Cinema*. New York: Cape & Harrison Smith, 1930.

Sarris, Andrew. *'You Ain't Heard Nothin' Yet': the American Talking Film – History and Memory 1927–1949*. New York: Oxford University Press, 1998.

Schwartz, Nancy Lynn. *The Hollywood Writers' Wars*. New York: Knopf, 1982.

Sheeran, Patrick F. *The Novels of Liam O'Flaherty: a Study in Romantic Realism*. Atlantic Highlands, NJ: Humanities Press, 1976.

Smith, James L. *Melodrama*. London: Methuen, 1977.

Spiegel, Alan. *Visual Consciousness in Film and the Modern Novel*. Charlottesville: University Press of Virginia, 1976.

Theweleit, Klaus. *Male Fantasies*. Minneapolis: University of Minnesota Press, 1990.

Vanloo, Rolf E., and Artur (*sic*) Robison. *'The Informer (Die Nacht nach dem Verrat*), freely adapted from the novel by Liam O'Flaherty'. Screenplay (1928). Irish Film Institute Ms.